Quizz islam

QUESTIONS

1) What does «Islam» mean?

A. Peace, submission, obedience (to God)
B. Arab
C. Religion
D. Planet

2) Who is a Muslim?

A. An Arabic
B. A person who lives in an Arab country
C. Someone who practices Islam
D. A Maghrebian

3) Allah ﷻ is ... ?

A. Single
B. Three
C. Two
D. Three in one!

4) How can we describe the existence of Allah ﷻ?

A. Without beginning, with an end
B. Without beginning or end
C. With a beginning, without an end
D. With a beginning and an end

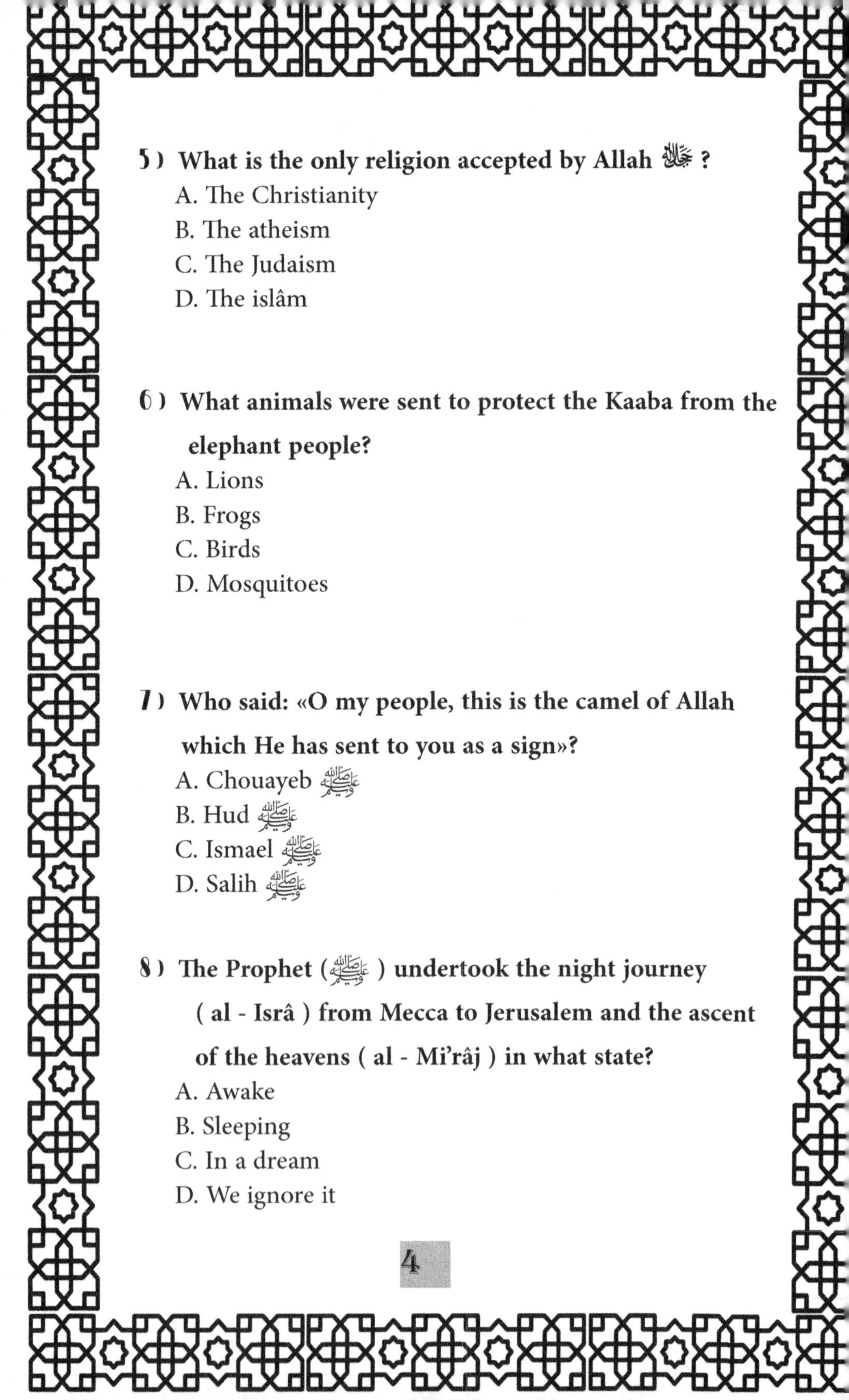

5) What is the only religion accepted by Allah ﷻ ?

A. The Christianity

B. The atheism

C. The Judaism

D. The islâm

6) What animals were sent to protect the Kaaba from the elephant people?

A. Lions

B. Frogs

C. Birds

D. Mosquitoes

7) Who said: «O my people, this is the camel of Allah which He has sent to you as a sign»?

A. Chouayeb ﷺ

B. Hud ﷺ

C. Ismael ﷺ

D. Salih ﷺ

8) The Prophet (ﷺ) undertook the night journey (al - Isrâ) from Mecca to Jerusalem and the ascent of the heavens (al - Mi'râj) in what state?

A. Awake

B. Sleeping

C. In a dream

D. We ignore it

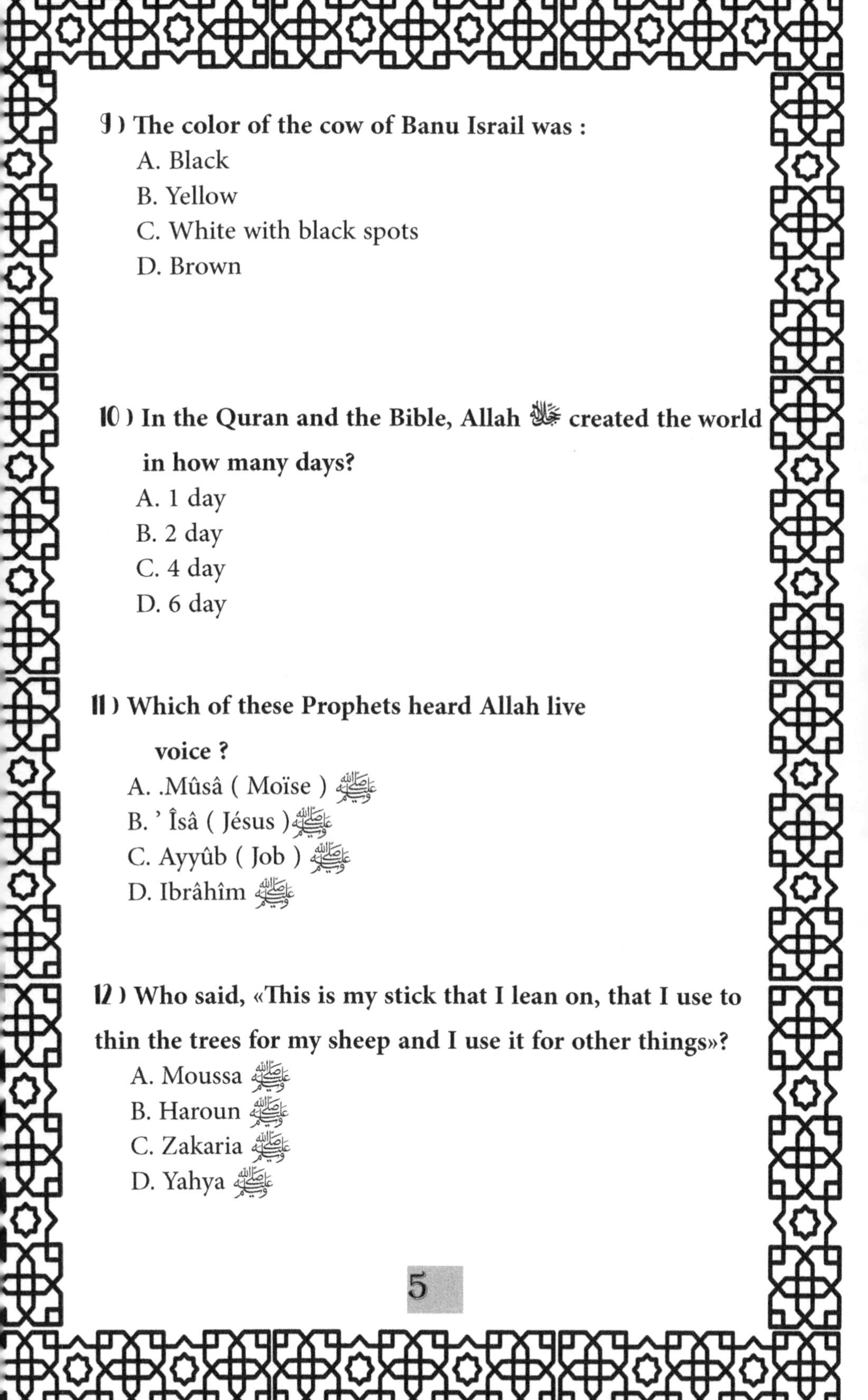

9) The color of the cow of Banu Israil was :

A. Black
B. Yellow
C. White with black spots
D. Brown

10) In the Quran and the Bible, Allah ﷻ created the world in how many days?

A. 1 day
B. 2 day
C. 4 day
D. 6 day

11) Which of these Prophets heard Allah live voice ?

A. .Mûsâ (Moïse) ﷺ
B. ' Îsâ (Jésus)ﷺ
C. Ayyûb (Job) ﷺ
D. Ibrâhîm ﷺ

12) Who said, «This is my stick that I lean on, that I use to thin the trees for my sheep and I use it for other things»?

A. Moussa ﷺ
B. Haroun ﷺ
C. Zakaria ﷺ
D. Yahya ﷺ

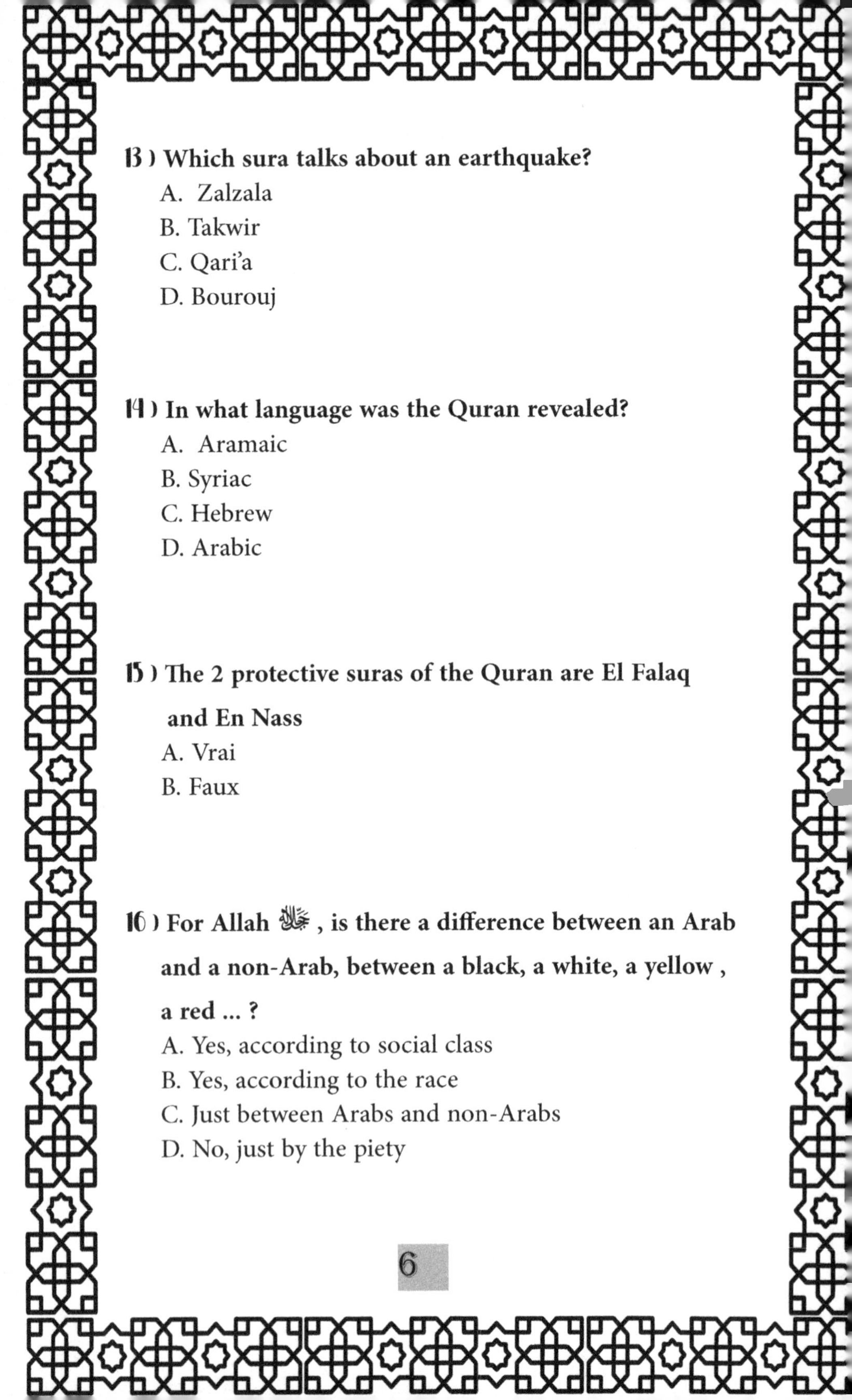

13) Which sura talks about an earthquake?

A. Zalzala
B. Takwir
C. Qari'a
D. Bourouj

14) In what language was the Quran revealed?

A. Aramaic
B. Syriac
C. Hebrew
D. Arabic

15) The 2 protective suras of the Quran are El Falaq and En Nass

A. Vrai
B. Faux

16) For Allah ﷻ , is there a difference between an Arab and a non-Arab, between a black, a white, a yellow , a red ... ?

A. Yes, according to social class
B. Yes, according to the race
C. Just between Arabs and non-Arabs
D. No, just by the piety

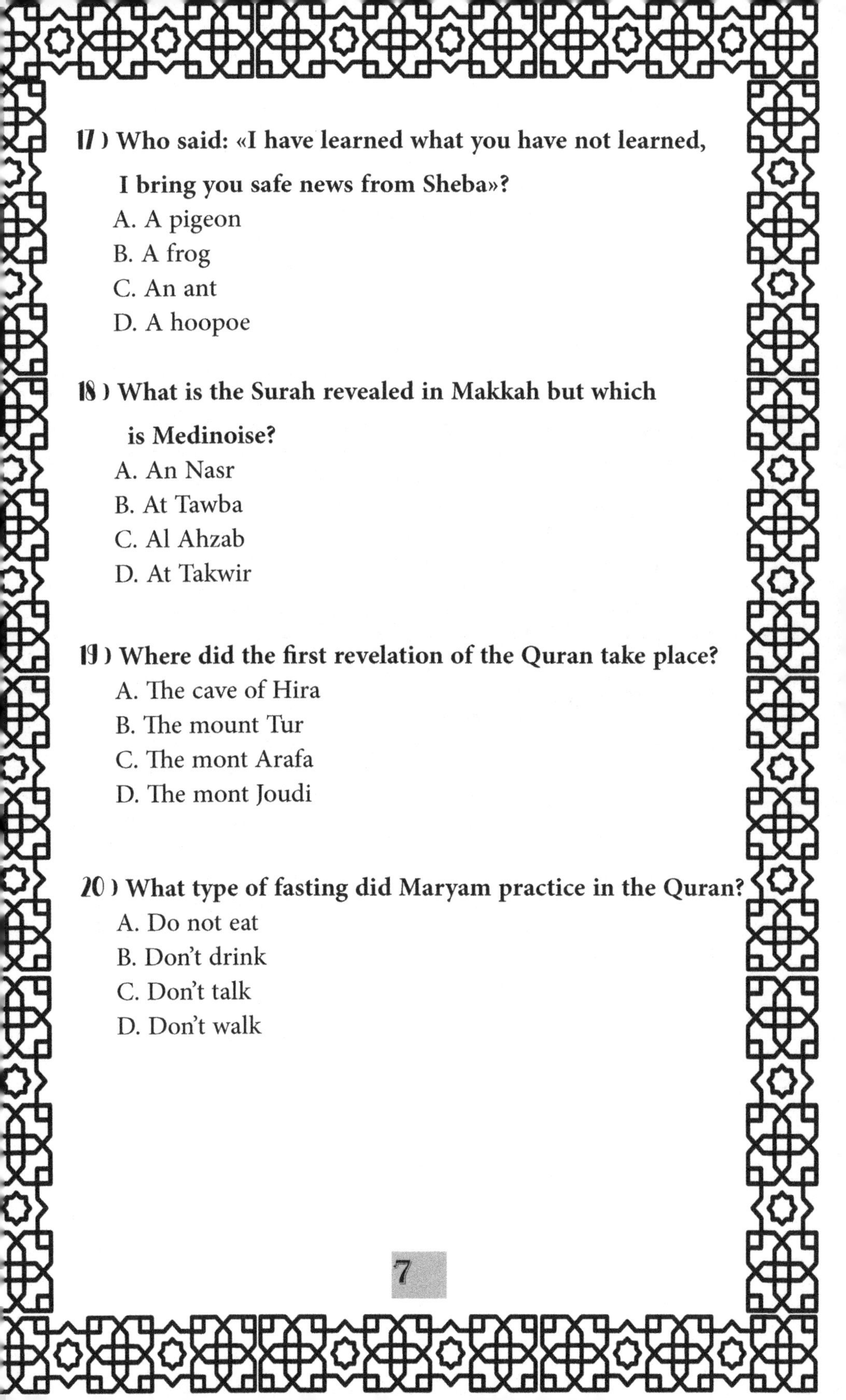

17) Who said: «I have learned what you have not learned, I bring you safe news from Sheba»?

A. A pigeon
B. A frog
C. An ant
D. A hoopoe

18) What is the Surah revealed in Makkah but which is Medinoise?

A. An Nasr
B. At Tawba
C. Al Ahzab
D. At Takwir

19) Where did the first revelation of the Quran take place?

A. The cave of Hira
B. The mount Tur
C. The mont Arafa
D. The mont Joudi

20) What type of fasting did Maryam practice in the Quran?

A. Do not eat
B. Don't drink
C. Don't talk
D. Don't walk

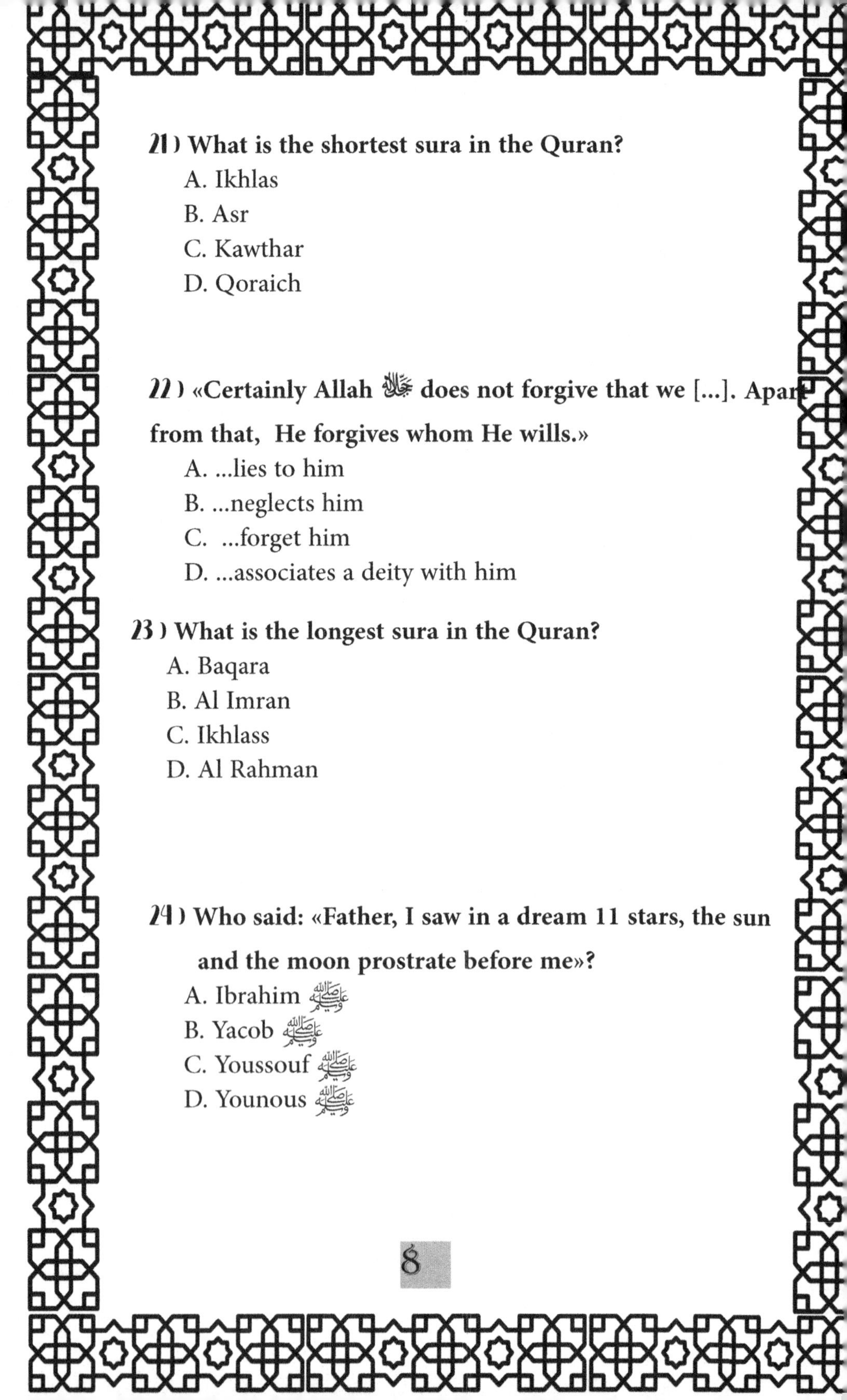

21) What is the shortest sura in the Quran?

A. Ikhlas
B. Asr
C. Kawthar
D. Qoraich

22) «Certainly Allah ﷻ does not forgive that we [...]. Apart from that, He forgives whom He wills.»

A. ...lies to him
B. ...neglects him
C. ...forget him
D. ...associates a deity with him

23) What is the longest sura in the Quran?

A. Baqara
B. Al Imran
C. Ikhlass
D. Al Rahman

24) Who said: «Father, I saw in a dream 11 stars, the sun and the moon prostrate before me»?

A. Ibrahim ﷺ
B. Yacob ﷺ
C. Youssouf ﷺ
D. Younous ﷺ

25) In Surah Al-Kahf, the servant of Moses ﷺ forgets Something on the way, what is it?

A. His bag
B. A fish
C. A stick
D. Bread

26) The Quran consists of how many suras?

A. 110
B. 112
C. 114
D. 116

27) How Indonesia became Muslim?

A. By war
B. By Muslim books
C. By Muslim traders
D. By philosophers

28) What was the qunia (surname) of the Prophet ﷺ?

A. Aboul Qasim
B. Ibn Abdallah
C. Abou Fatima
D. Ibn Abou Talib

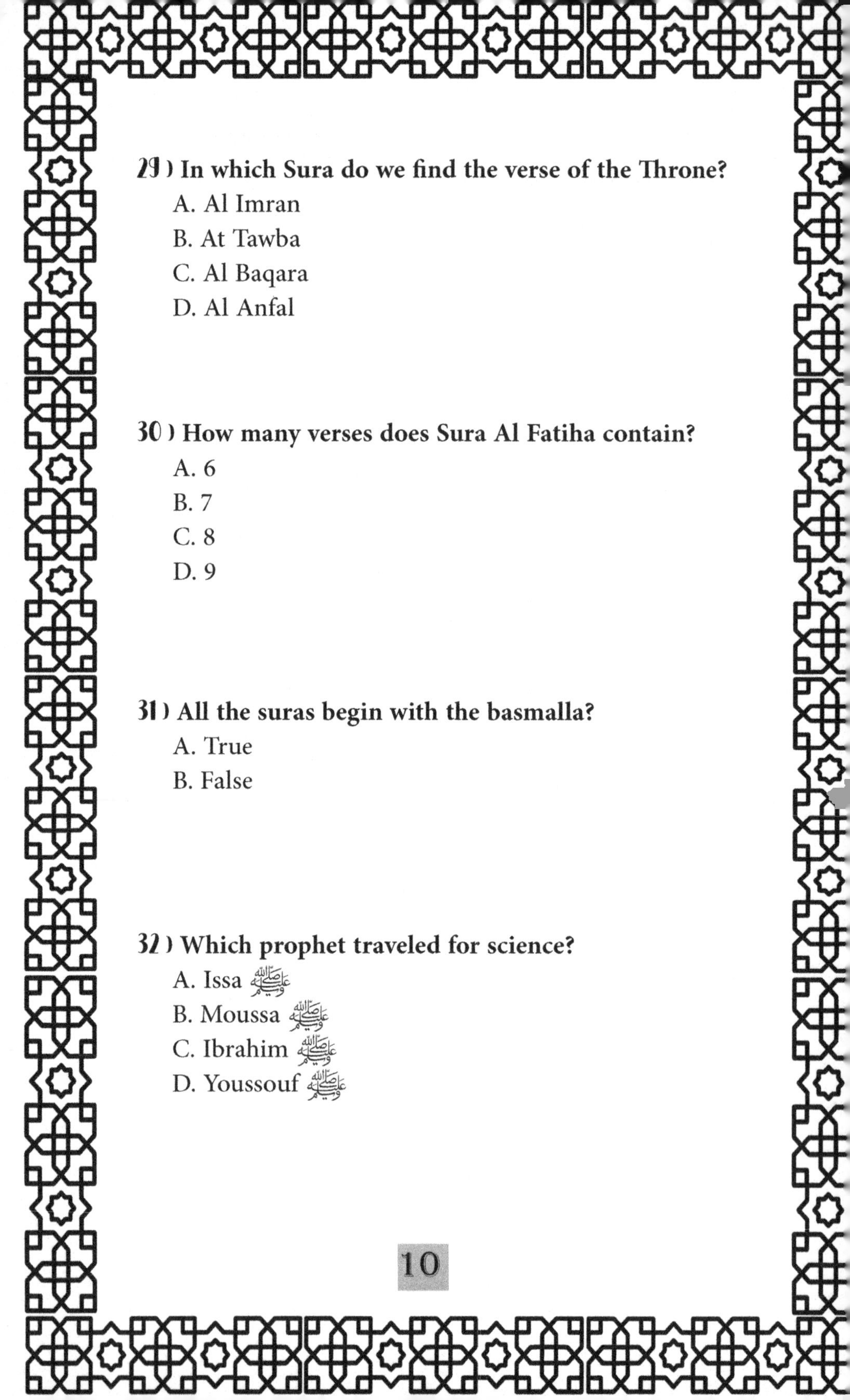

29) In which Sura do we find the verse of the Throne?

A. Al Imran
B. At Tawba
C. Al Baqara
D. Al Anfal

30) How many verses does Sura Al Fatiha contain?

A. 6
B. 7
C. 8
D. 9

31) All the suras begin with the basmalla?

A. True
B. False

32) Which prophet traveled for science?

A. Issa ﷺ
B. Moussa ﷺ
C. Ibrahim ﷺ
D. Youssouf ﷺ

33) Dry ablutions (tayamoum) can be performed if:

A. Water is too hot
B. If no water is available
C. To avoid becoming wet
D. To gain time

34) How long did the revelation of the Koran last in Medina?

A. 10 ans
B. 13 ans
C. 23 ans
D. 12 ans

35) Which sura speaks of a river of paradise?

A. Ar Rahman
B. Al Waqi'a
C. Al Kawthar
D. Al Ikhlas

36) Which sura refers to the battle of Ohud?

A. Anfal
B. Imran
C. Ahzab
D. Tawba

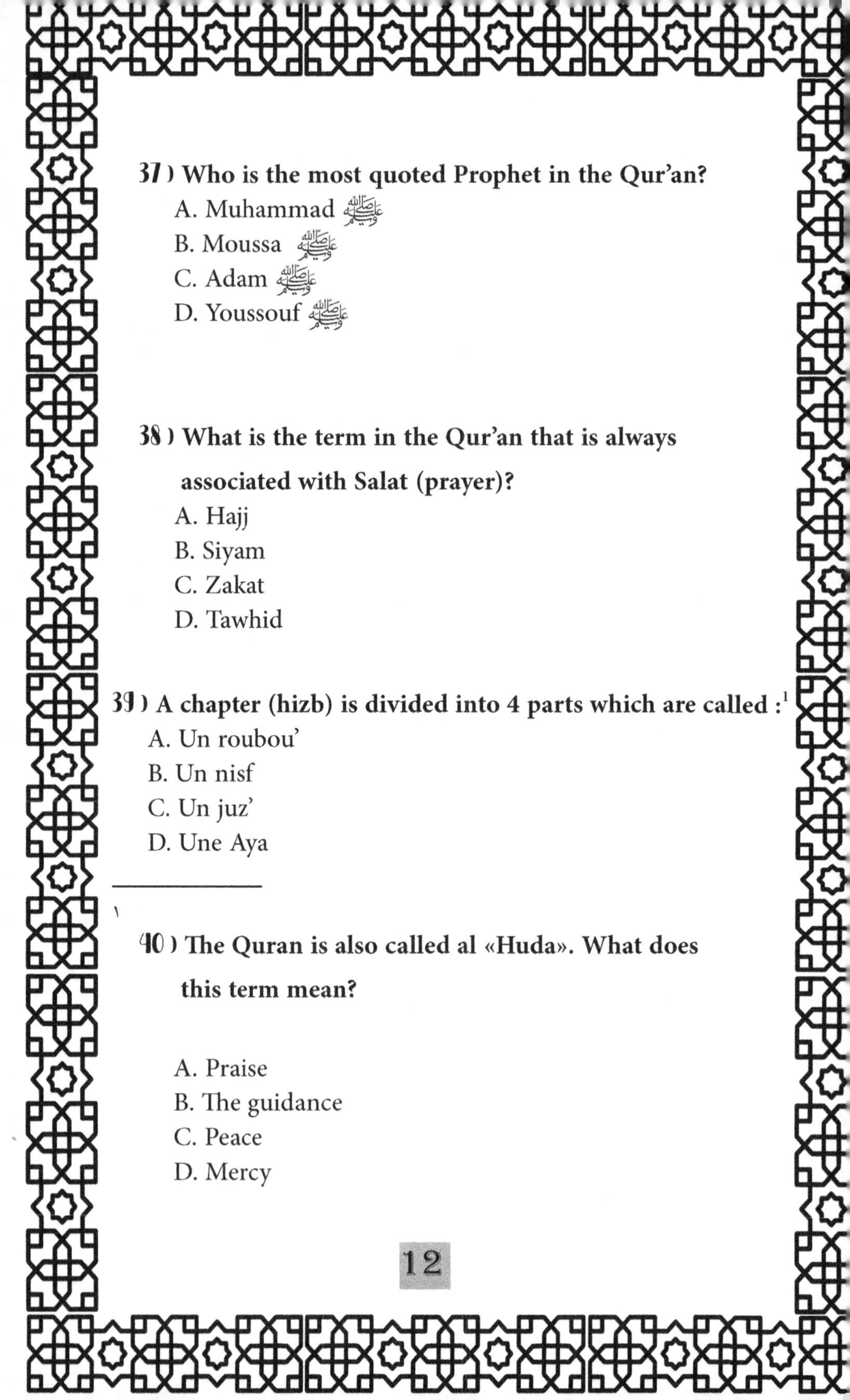

37) Who is the most quoted Prophet in the Qur'an?

A. Muhammad ﷺ
B. Moussa ﷺ
C. Adam ﷺ
D. Youssouf ﷺ

38) What is the term in the Qur'an that is always associated with Salat (prayer)?

A. Hajj
B. Siyam
C. Zakat
D. Tawhid

39) A chapter (hizb) is divided into 4 parts which are called :[1]

A. Un roubou'
B. Un nisf
C. Un juz'
D. Une Aya

١

40) The Quran is also called al «Huda». What does this term mean?

A. Praise
B. The guidance
C. Peace
D. Mercy

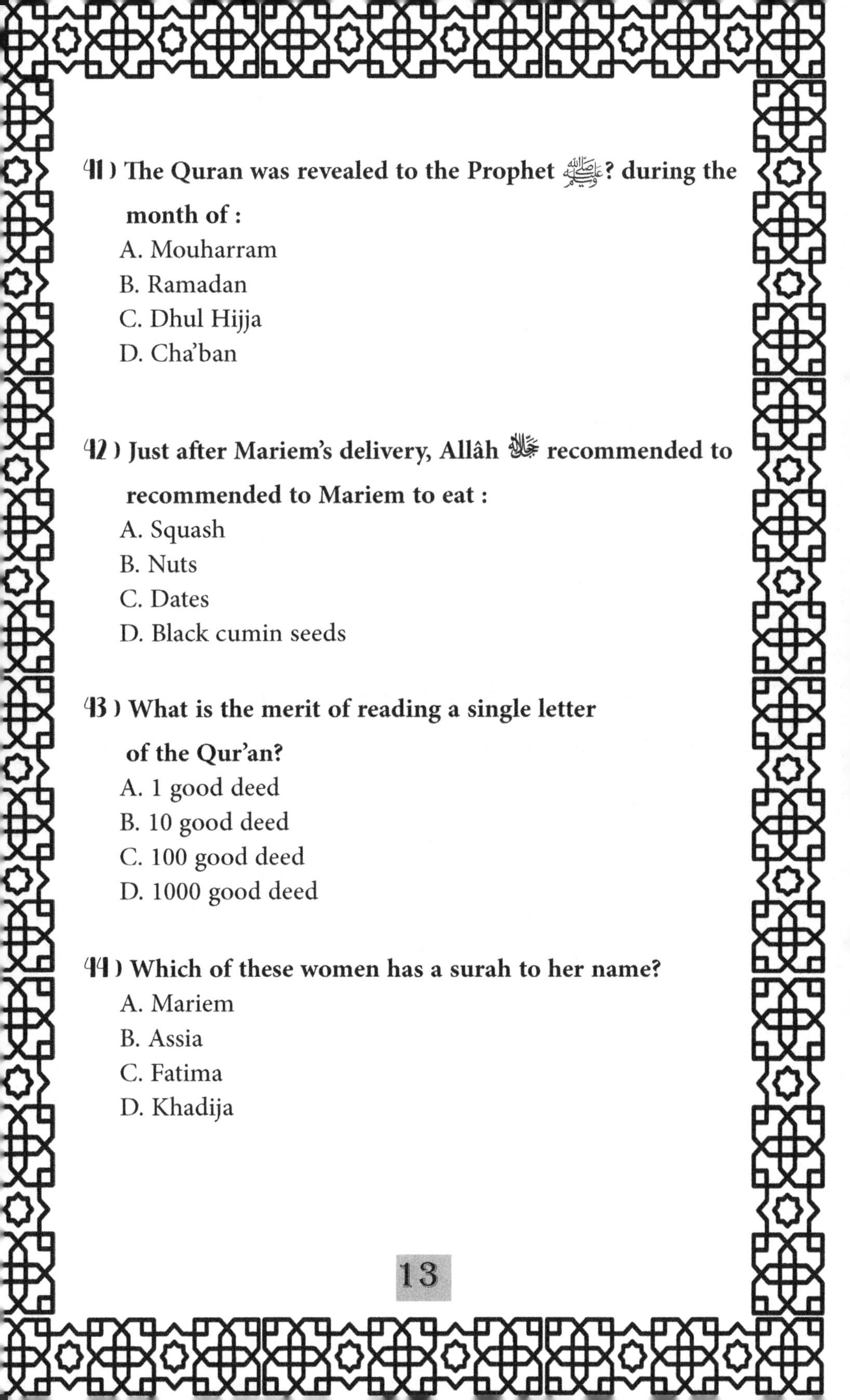

41) The Quran was revealed to the Prophet ﷺ? during the month of :

A. Mouharram
B. Ramadan
C. Dhul Hijja
D. Cha'ban

42) Just after Mariem's delivery, Allâh جل جلاله recommended to recommended to Mariem to eat :

A. Squash
B. Nuts
C. Dates
D. Black cumin seeds

43) What is the merit of reading a single letter of the Qur'an?

A. 1 good deed
B. 10 good deed
C. 100 good deed
D. 1000 good deed

44) Which of these women has a surah to her name?

A. Mariem
B. Assia
C. Fatima
D. Khadija

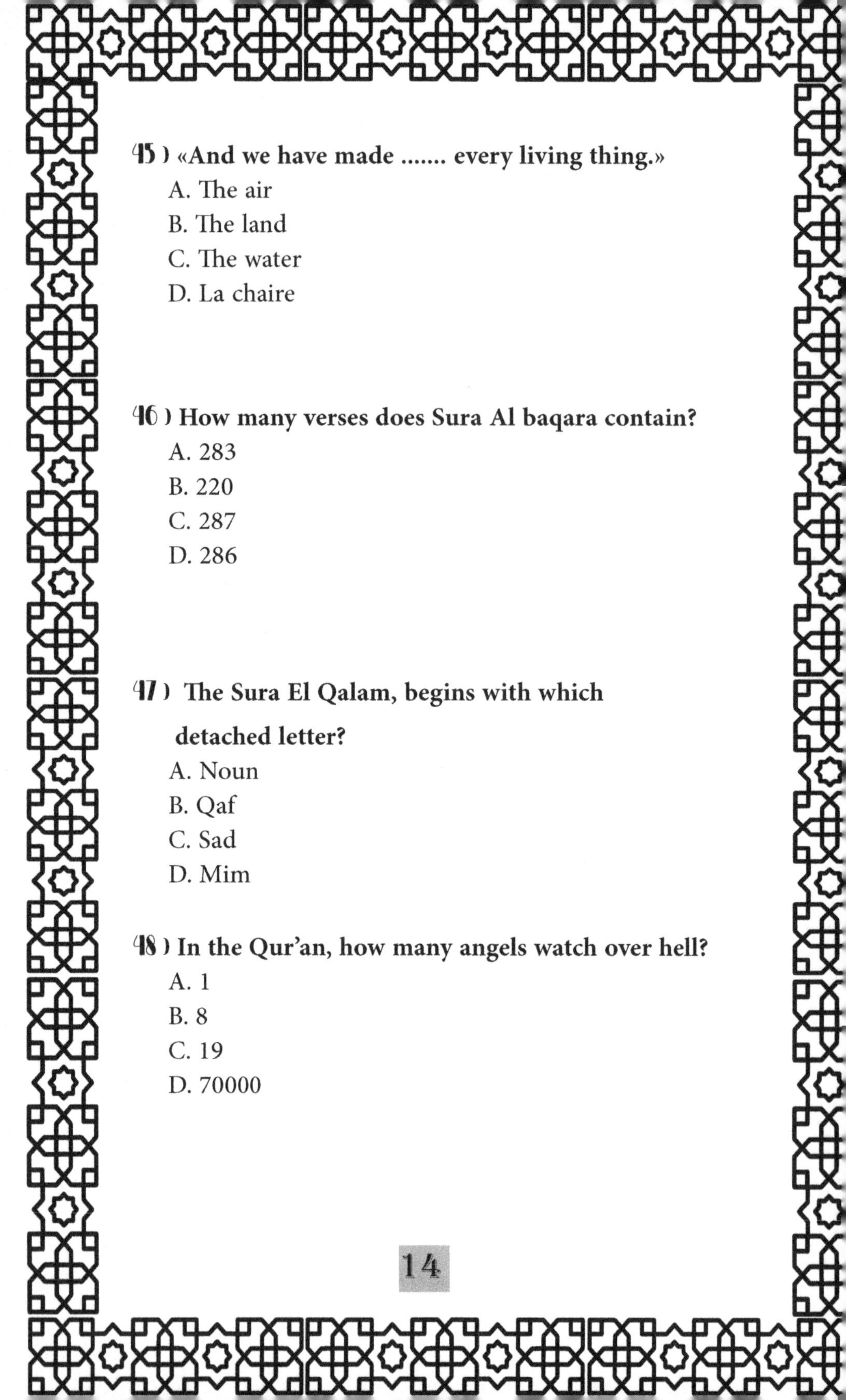

45) «And we have made .... every living thing.»

A. The air
B. The land
C. The water
D. La chaire

46) How many verses does Sura Al baqara contain?

A. 283
B. 220
C. 287
D. 286

47) The Sura El Qalam, begins with which detached letter?

A. Noun
B. Qaf
C. Sad
D. Mim

48) In the Qur'an, how many angels watch over hell?

A. 1
B. 8
C. 19
D. 70000

49) In which Sura is it written: «We have certainly created man in the most created man in the most perfect form»?

A. Adhesion
B. The opening
C. The fig
D. The man

50) In Surah Al Kahf, which animal accompanied the boys who took refuge in the cave ?

A. A Cat
B. A sheep
C. A dog
D. A goat

51) Is there a sura named after the Prophet Nuh ﷺ ?

A. Yes
B. No

52) What animal is not a miracle of Allah ﷻ ?

A. The camel of Salih
B. The sheep of Ibrahim
C. The serpent of Moses
D. The ant of Souleyman

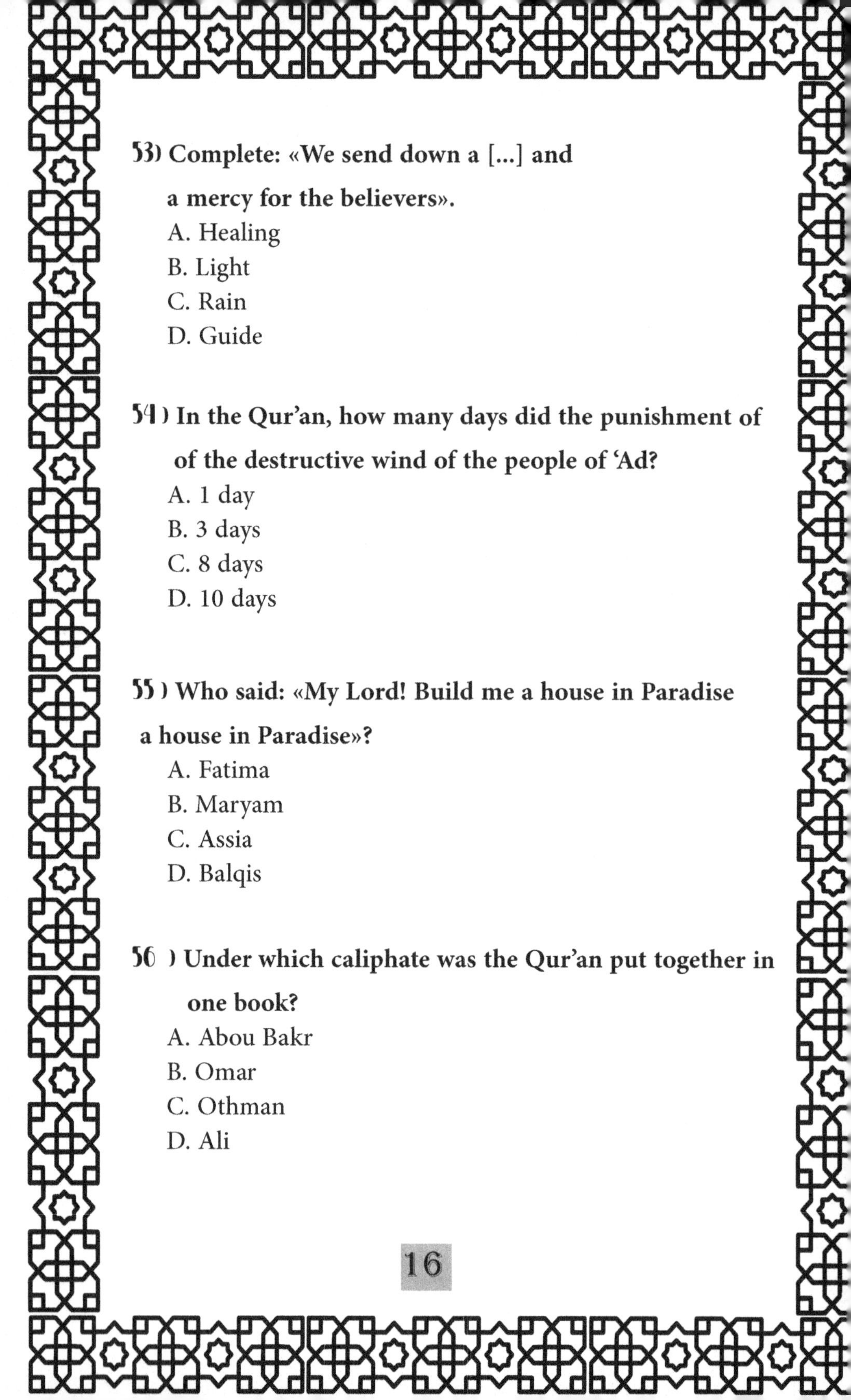

53) Complete: «We send down a [...] and a mercy for the believers».

A. Healing
B. Light
C. Rain
D. Guide

54) In the Qur'an, how many days did the punishment of of the destructive wind of the people of 'Ad?

A. 1 day
B. 3 days
C. 8 days
D. 10 days

55) Who said: «My Lord! Build me a house in Paradise a house in Paradise»?

A. Fatima
B. Maryam
C. Assia
D. Balqis

56) Under which caliphate was the Qur'an put together in one book?

A. Abou Bakr
B. Omar
C. Othman
D. Ali

57) In the Koran, which are the 2 angels descended on Babylon?

A. Munkar and Nakir
B. Harut and Marut
C. Djibril and Mikail
D. Malik and Israfil

58) What is the mother of cities in the Qur'an?

A. Mecca
B. Jérusalem
C. Medina
D. Constantinople

59) Who refused to bow down to Adam ﷺ?

A. Eve
B. Iblis
C. The snake
D. The sky

60) How were the people of the 'Ad destroyed?

A. An earthquake
B. A deluge
C. A windstorm
D. A dreadful cry

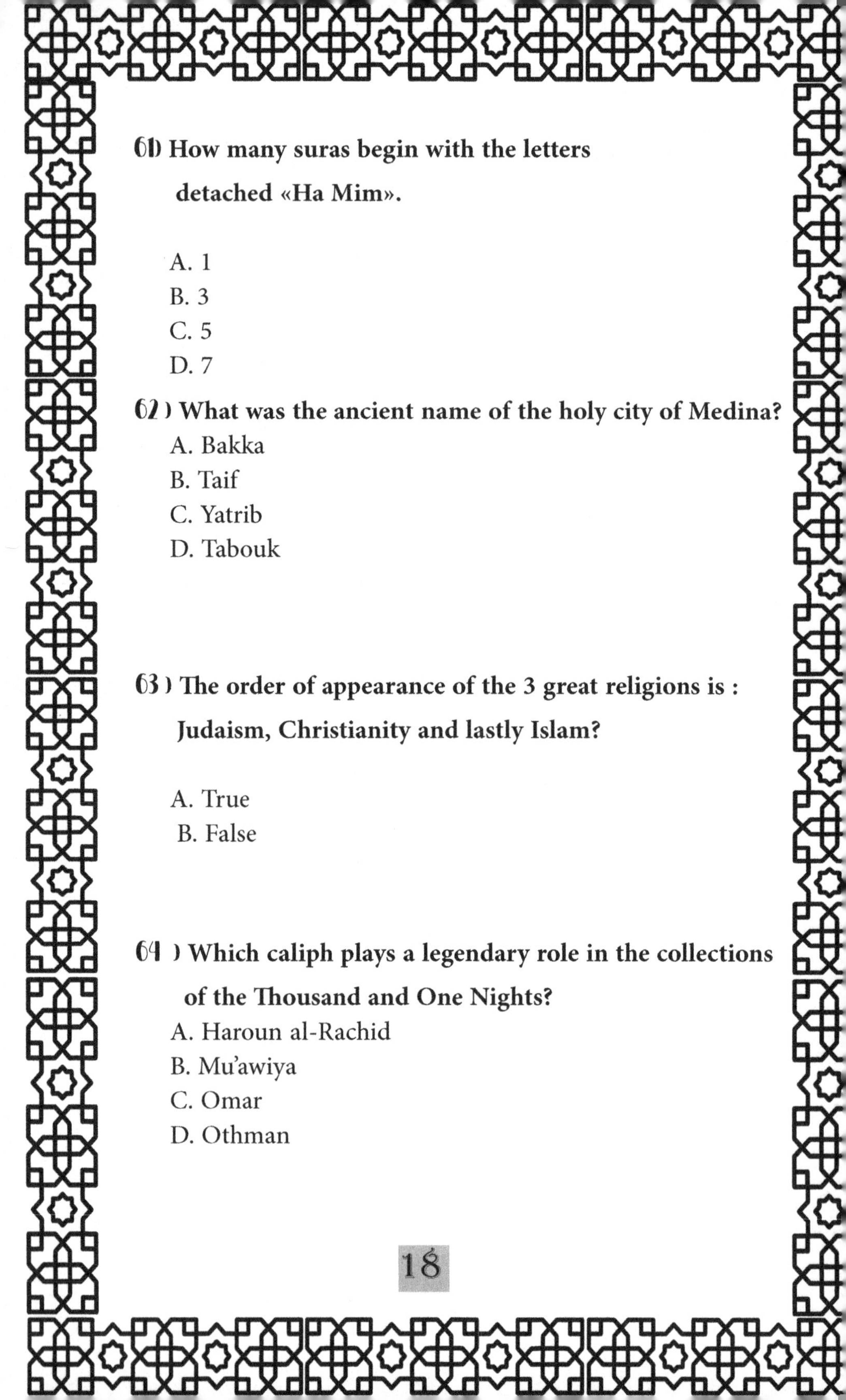

61) How many suras begin with the letters detached «Ha Mim».

A. 1
B. 3
C. 5
D. 7

62) What was the ancient name of the holy city of Medina?

A. Bakka
B. Taif
C. Yatrib
D. Tabouk

63) The order of appearance of the 3 great religions is : Judaism, Christianity and lastly Islam?

A. True
B. False

64) Which caliph plays a legendary role in the collections of the Thousand and One Nights?

A. Haroun al-Rachid
B. Mu'awiya
C. Omar
D. Othman

65) What was the name of the Abyssinian general who wanted destroy Mecca with an elephant?

A. Leclerc
B. Patton
C. Harmel
D. Abraha

66) During the Abbasid dynasty, which people destroyed the capital Baghdad?

A. The Crusaders
B. The Chinese
C. The Mongols
D. The visigoths

67) What is the name of the famous doctor and philosopher Muslim who is called Avicenna in the West?

A. Ibn Ruchd
B. Ibn Tofail
C. Ibn Fernes
D. Ibn Sina

68) Which French king received a famous clock from the Caliph Haroun Rachid?

A. Clovis
B. Dagobert
C. Charlemagne
D. Pépin Le Bref

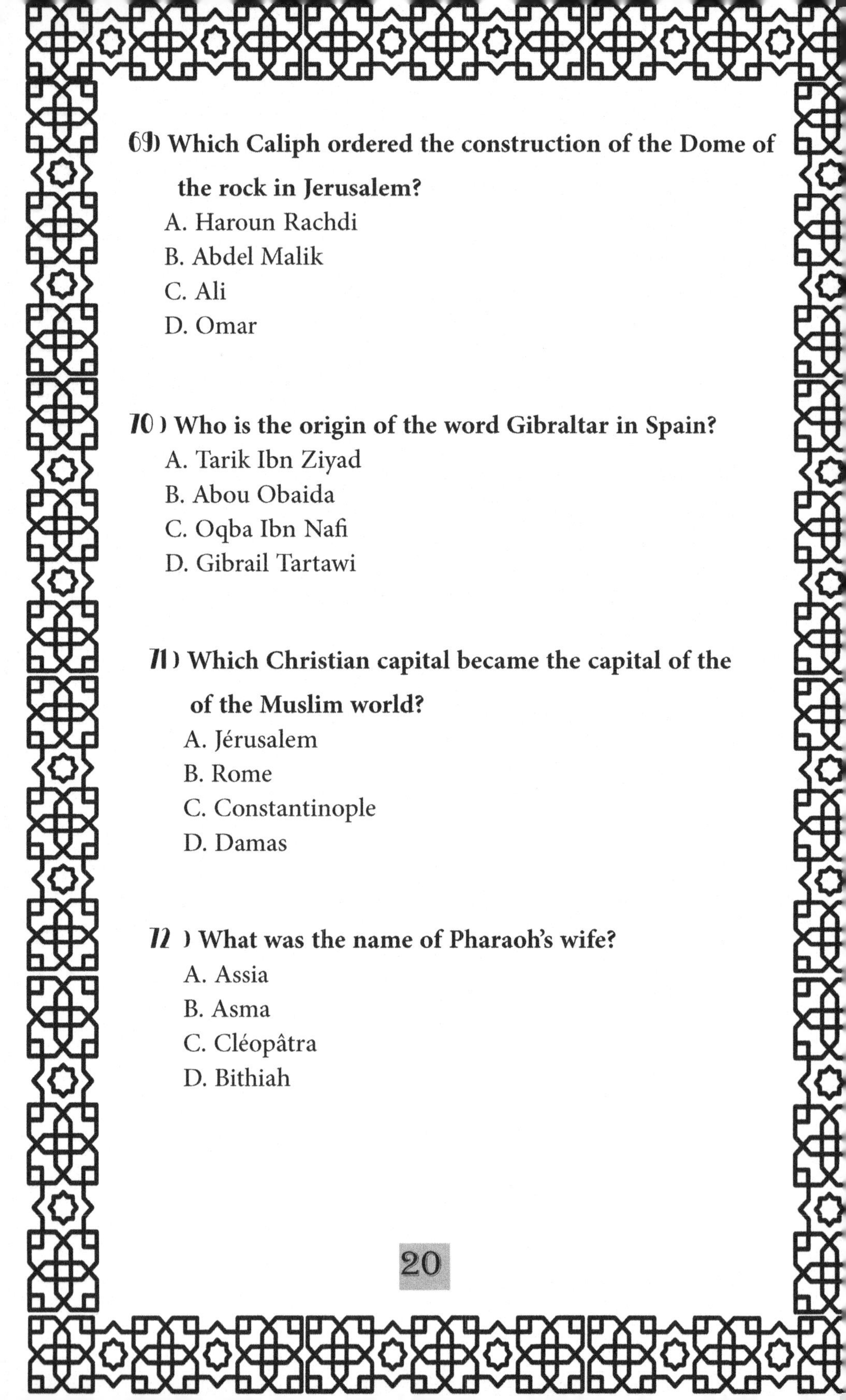

69) Which Caliph ordered the construction of the Dome of the rock in Jerusalem?

A. Haroun Rachdi
B. Abdel Malik
C. Ali
D. Omar

70) Who is the origin of the word Gibraltar in Spain?

A. Tarik Ibn Ziyad
B. Abou Obaida
C. Oqba Ibn Nafi
D. Gibrail Tartawi

71) Which Christian capital became the capital of the of the Muslim world?

A. Jérusalem
B. Rome
C. Constantinople
D. Damas

72) What was the name of Pharaoh's wife?

A. Assia
B. Asma
C. Cléopâtra
D. Bithiah

13) The region that was called Al Ifriqiya is called today :

A. Tunis
B. Alger
C. Marrakech
D. Dakar

14) At the time of the Prophet ?, the dirham was made of silver and the dinar in gold?

A. True
B. False

15) Is there a sura named «Muhammad» in the Quran?

A. Yes
B. No

16) When clothes were offered to the Prophet ﷺ? he [...]

A. gave a gift
B. he greeted with a hug.
C. was wearing it
D. gave it back

77) What was the name of the Prophet's father ﷺ?

A. Abdallah

B. Abd Mottalib

C. Abou Talib

D. Ismail

78) How old was the Prophet Muhammad ﷺ when his mother passed away?

A. 1 year

B. 3 years

C. 5 years

D. 6 years

79) The mother of the Prophet ﷺ was called ?

A. Amina

B. Halima

C. Maryam

D. Assia

80) Where did the Prophet ﷺ die?

A. In the war

B. In Mecca

C. At Aicha's house

D. At the hospital

81) The Prophet Muhammad ﷺ is the last of the prophets?

A. True
B. False

82) What was the surname of the prophet Muhammad ﷺ before Islam?

A. The good man
B. The trustworthy one (The reliable one)
C. The generous one
D. The strong man

83) The Prophet Muhammad ﷺ died at what age?

A. 43 years old
B. 53 years old
C. 63 years old
D. 73 years old

84) The Prophet ﷺ died in :

A. 632
B. 1632
C. 1857
D. 200

85) Did the Prophet ﷺ have brothers and sisters?

A. True
B. False

86) Prophet Muhammad ﷺ was born in the year :

A. Of the dragon
B. Of the Tiger
C. Of the Sheep
D. Of the Elephant

87) At what age did the Prophet ﷺ receive the revelation?

A. 30 years
B. 40 years
C. 50 years
D. 60 years

88) When he arrived in Medina, the Prophet ﷺ prayed towards which direction?

A. Mecca
B. Medina
C. El Quds
D. The sky

89) Was the Prophet ﷺ sent only for the Arabs?

A. True
B. False

90) What was the first action of the Prophet ﷺ in Medina?

A. Establishment of a Muslim market
B. Fraternizing the Muhajirin and the Ansar
C. A peace pact with the different tribes
D. Building a mosque

91) The Prophet ﷺ had:

A. 4 daughters and 3 sons
B. 4 daughters and 2 sons
C. 4 daughters
D. 4 sons

92) What is the daughter of the Prophet ﷺ of whom he said: «Do you not accept to be the princess of the women of Paradise or of the women of the believers?»

A. Roqayya
B. Zayneb
C. Fatima
D. Oum Kalthoum

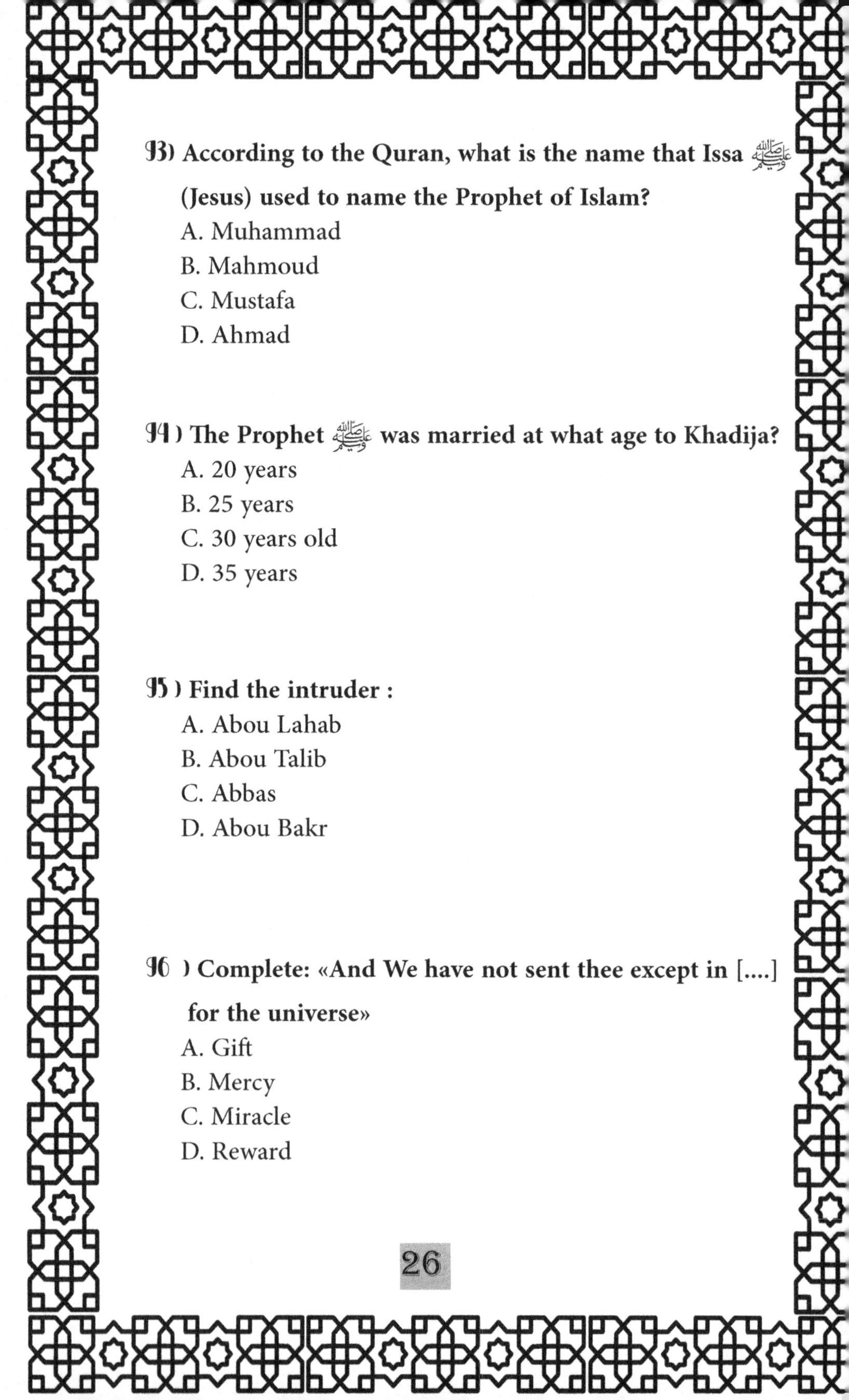

93) According to the Quran, what is the name that Issa ﷺ (Jesus) used to name the Prophet of Islam?

A. Muhammad
B. Mahmoud
C. Mustafa
D. Ahmad

94) The Prophet ﷺ was married at what age to Khadija?

A. 20 years
B. 25 years
C. 30 years old
D. 35 years

95) Find the intruder :

A. Abou Lahab
B. Abou Talib
C. Abbas
D. Abou Bakr

96) Complete: «And We have not sent thee except in [....] for the universe»

A. Gift
B. Mercy
C. Miracle
D. Reward

97) The Prophet ﷺ used to ask Allah for forgiveness more than [...] a day

A. 10
B. 70
C. 100
D. 1000

98) The secret preaching of the Prophet ﷺ Psl in Mecca lasted :

A. 3 years
B. 7 years
C. 1 year
D. 10 years

99) What is the name of the people who welcomed the Prophet ﷺ in Medina?

A. Quraych
B. Ansars
C. Banu Nadir
D. Banu Ghatafan

100) Is it permissible to advance the payment of his Zakat?

A. Yes, it is possible
B. No, it is not possible
C. Yes, but that the rich person who is afraid to spend it all
D. Yes, but the poor person who is afraid to spend it all

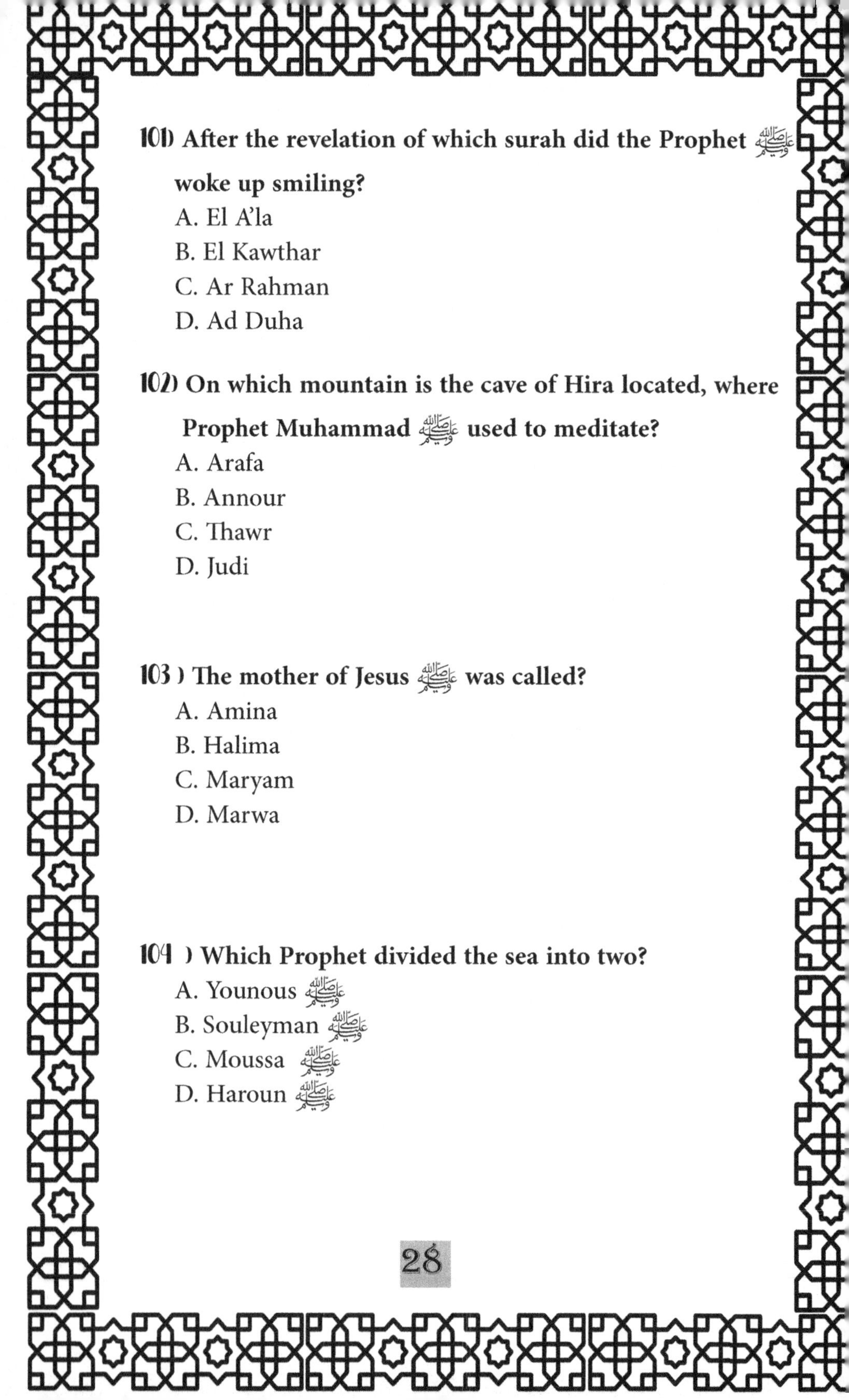

101) After the revelation of which surah did the Prophet ﷺ woke up smiling?

A. El A'la
B. El Kawthar
C. Ar Rahman
D. Ad Duha

102) On which mountain is the cave of Hira located, where Prophet Muhammad ﷺ used to meditate?

A. Arafa
B. Annour
C. Thawr
D. Judi

103) The mother of Jesus ﷺ was called?

A. Amina
B. Halima
C. Maryam
D. Marwa

104) Which Prophet divided the sea into two?

A. Younous ﷺ
B. Souleyman ﷺ
C. Moussa ﷺ
D. Haroun ﷺ

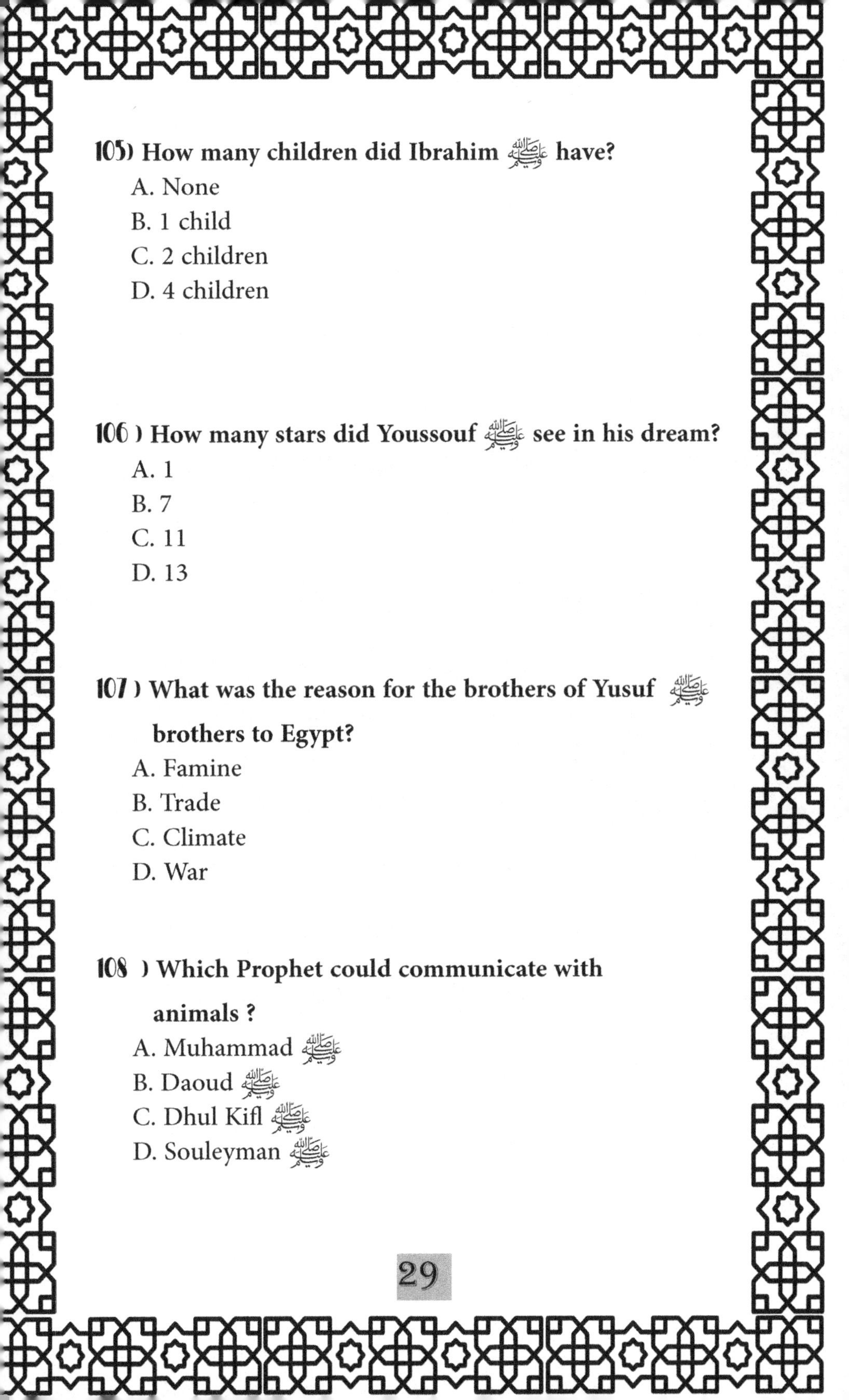

105) How many children did Ibrahim ﷺ have?

A. None

B. 1 child

C. 2 children

D. 4 children

106) How many stars did Youssouf ﷺ see in his dream?

A. 1

B. 7

C. 11

D. 13

107) What was the reason for the brothers of Yusuf ﷺ brothers to Egypt?

A. Famine

B. Trade

C. Climate

D. War

108) Which Prophet could communicate with animals ?

A. Muhammad ﷺ

B. Daoud ﷺ

C. Dhul Kifl ﷺ

D. Souleyman ﷺ

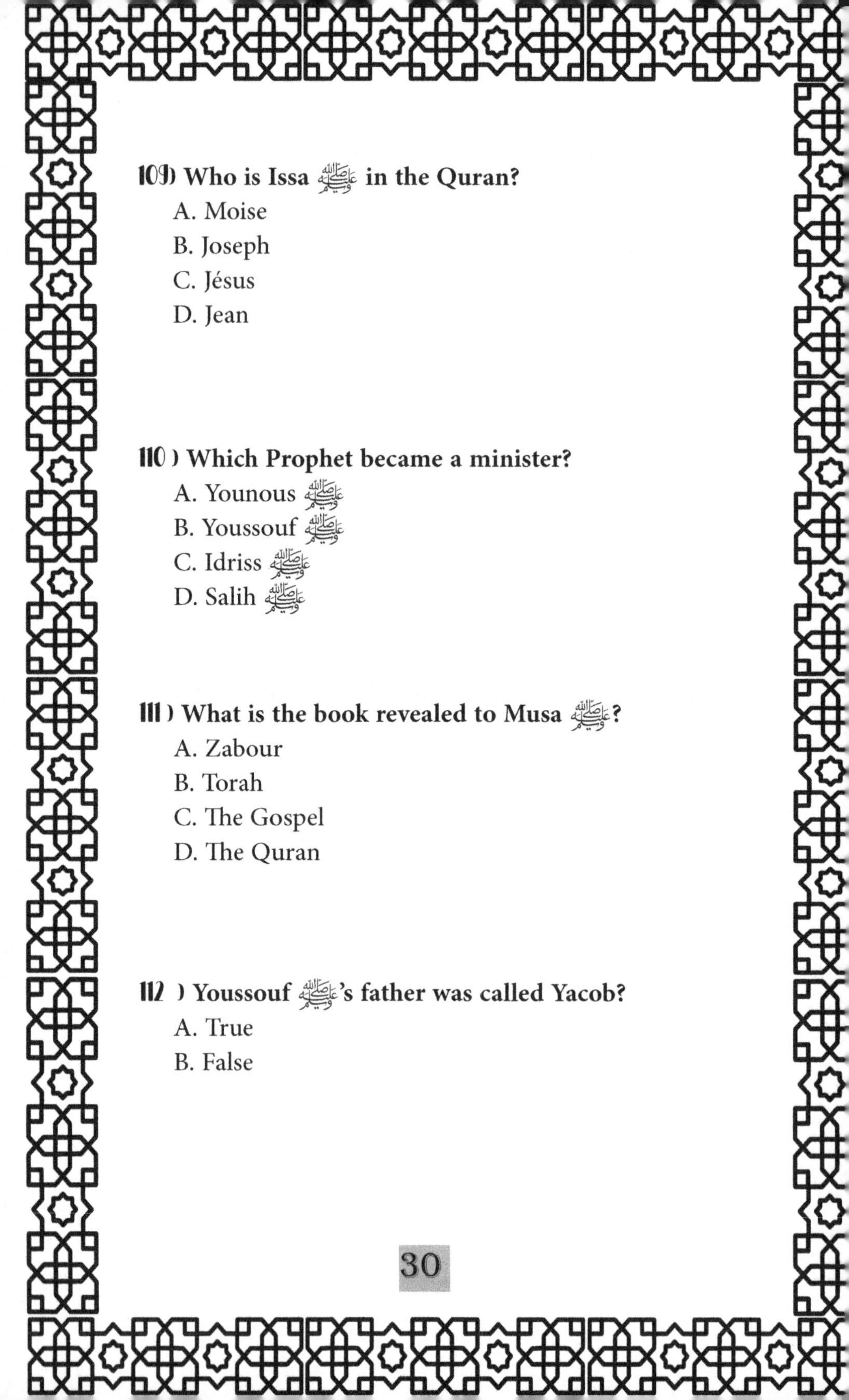

109) Who is Issa ﷺ in the Quran?

A. Moise
B. Joseph
C. Jésus
D. Jean

110) Which Prophet became a minister?

A. Younous ﷺ
B. Youssouf ﷺ
C. Idriss ﷺ
D. Salih ﷺ

111) What is the book revealed to Musa ﷺ?

A. Zabour
B. Torah
C. The Gospel
D. The Quran

112) Youssouf ﷺ's father was called Yacob?

A. True
B. False

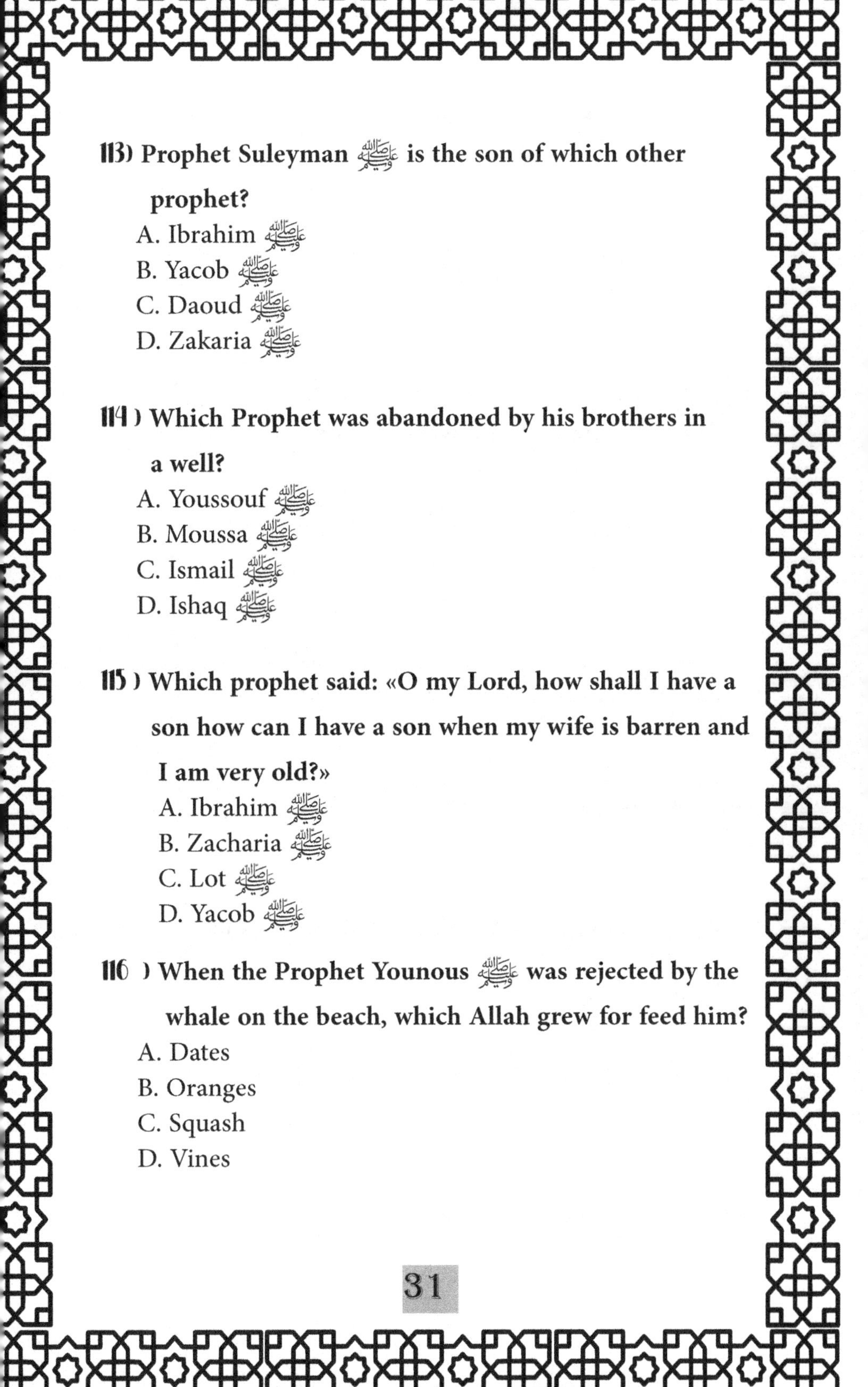

113) Prophet Suleyman ﷺ is the son of which other prophet?

A. Ibrahim ﷺ
B. Yacob ﷺ
C. Daoud ﷺ
D. Zakaria ﷺ

114) Which Prophet was abandoned by his brothers in a well?

A. Youssouf ﷺ
B. Moussa ﷺ
C. Ismail ﷺ
D. Ishaq ﷺ

115) Which prophet said: «O my Lord, how shall I have a son how can I have a son when my wife is barren and I am very old?»

A. Ibrahim ﷺ
B. Zacharia ﷺ
C. Lot ﷺ
D. Yacob ﷺ

116) When the Prophet Younous ﷺ was rejected by the whale on the beach, which Allah grew for feed him?

A. Dates
B. Oranges
C. Squash
D. Vines

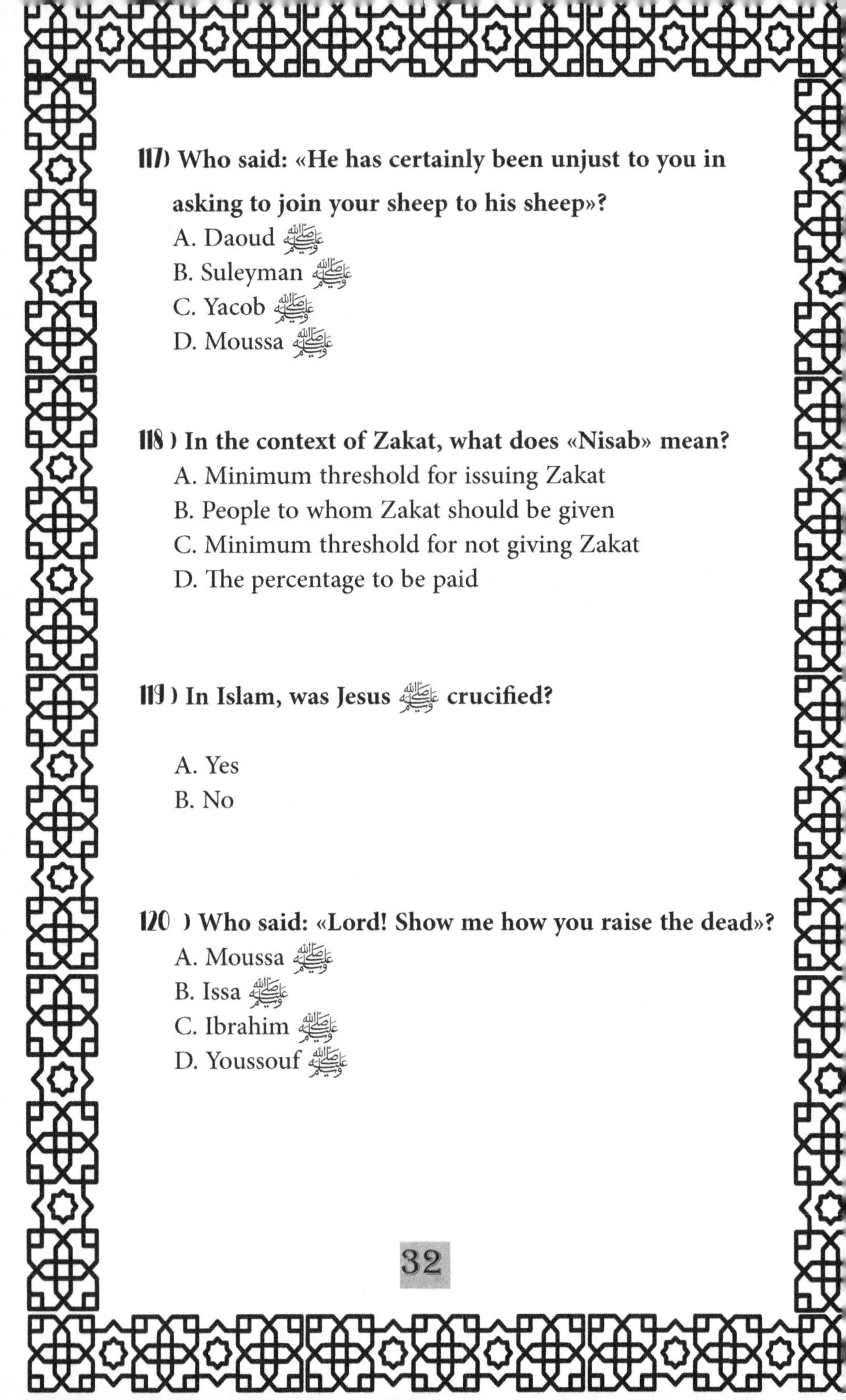

117) Who said: «He has certainly been unjust to you in asking to join your sheep to his sheep»?

A. Daoud ﷺ
B. Suleyman ﷺ
C. Yacob ﷺ
D. Moussa ﷺ

118) In the context of Zakat, what does «Nisab» mean?

A. Minimum threshold for issuing Zakat
B. People to whom Zakat should be given
C. Minimum threshold for not giving Zakat
D. The percentage to be paid

119) In Islam, was Jesus ﷺ crucified?

A. Yes
B. No

120) Who said: «Lord! Show me how you raise the dead»?

A. Moussa ﷺ
B. Issa ﷺ
C. Ibrahim ﷺ
D. Youssouf ﷺ

121) Which prophet was thrown into the fire by his own people?

A. Hud ﷺ
B. Elyes ﷺ
C. Idriss ﷺ
D. Ibrahim ﷺ

122) Who is the father of the Prophet Yahya ﷺ?

A. Yacob ﷺ
B. Ishaq ﷺ
C. Daoud ﷺ
D. Zacharia ﷺ

123) Who had the honour of looking after Maryam?

A. Zacharia ﷺ
B. Yahya ﷺ
C. Issa ﷺ
D. Sa mère

124) Ibrahim ﷺ had two wives, who are they?

A. Sephora and Sarah
B. Ester and Hajar
C. Sarah and Hajar
D. Hajar and Sephora

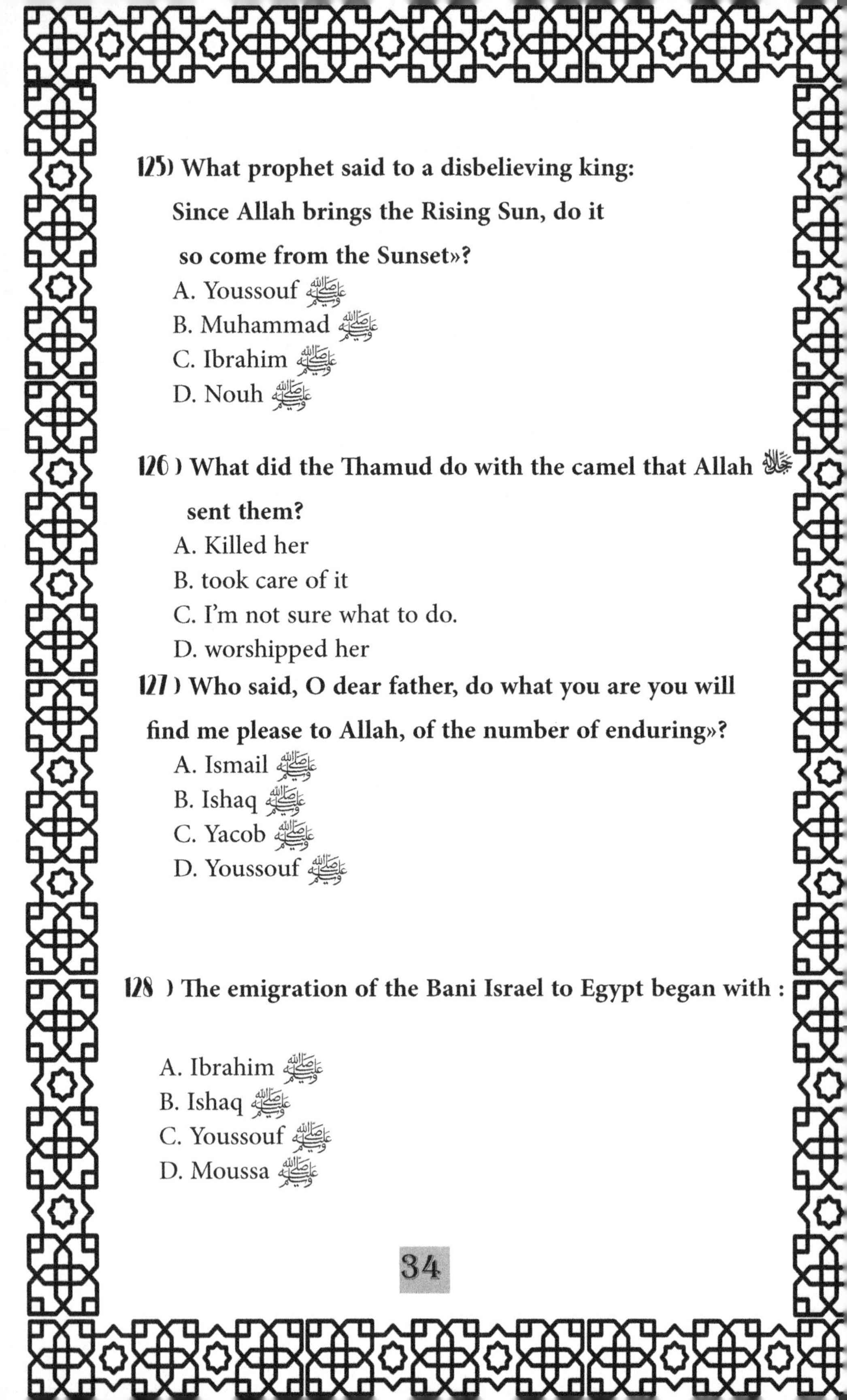

125) What prophet said to a disbelieving king: Since Allah brings the Rising Sun, do it so come from the Sunset»?

A. Youssouf ﷺ
B. Muhammad ﷺ
C. Ibrahim ﷺ
D. Nouh ﷺ

126) What did the Thamud do with the camel that Allah ﷻ sent them?

A. Killed her
B. took care of it
C. I'm not sure what to do.
D. worshipped her

127) Who said, O dear father, do what you are you will find me please to Allah, of the number of enduring»?

A. Ismail ﷺ
B. Ishaq ﷺ
C. Yacob ﷺ
D. Youssouf ﷺ

128) The emigration of the Bani Israel to Egypt began with :

A. Ibrahim ﷺ
B. Ishaq ﷺ
C. Youssouf ﷺ
D. Moussa ﷺ

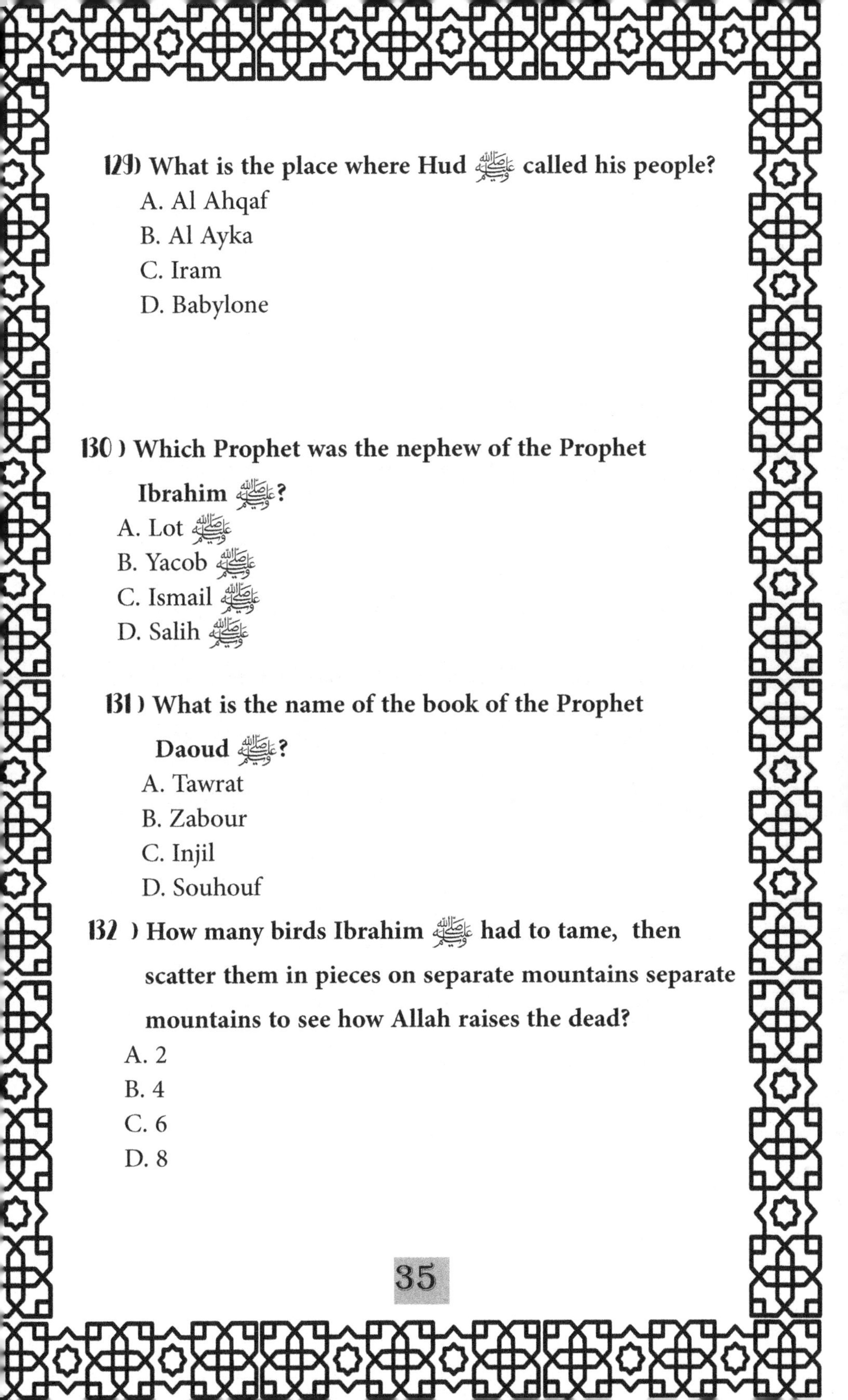

129) What is the place where Hud ﷺ called his people?

A. Al Ahqaf
B. Al Ayka
C. Iram
D. Babylone

130) Which Prophet was the nephew of the Prophet Ibrahim ﷺ?

A. Lot ﷺ
B. Yacob ﷺ
C. Ismail ﷺ
D. Salih ﷺ

131) What is the name of the book of the Prophet Daoud ﷺ?

A. Tawrat
B. Zabour
C. Injil
D. Souhouf

132) How many birds Ibrahim ﷺ had to tame, then scatter them in pieces on separate mountains separate mountains to see how Allah raises the dead?

A. 2
B. 4
C. 6
D. 8

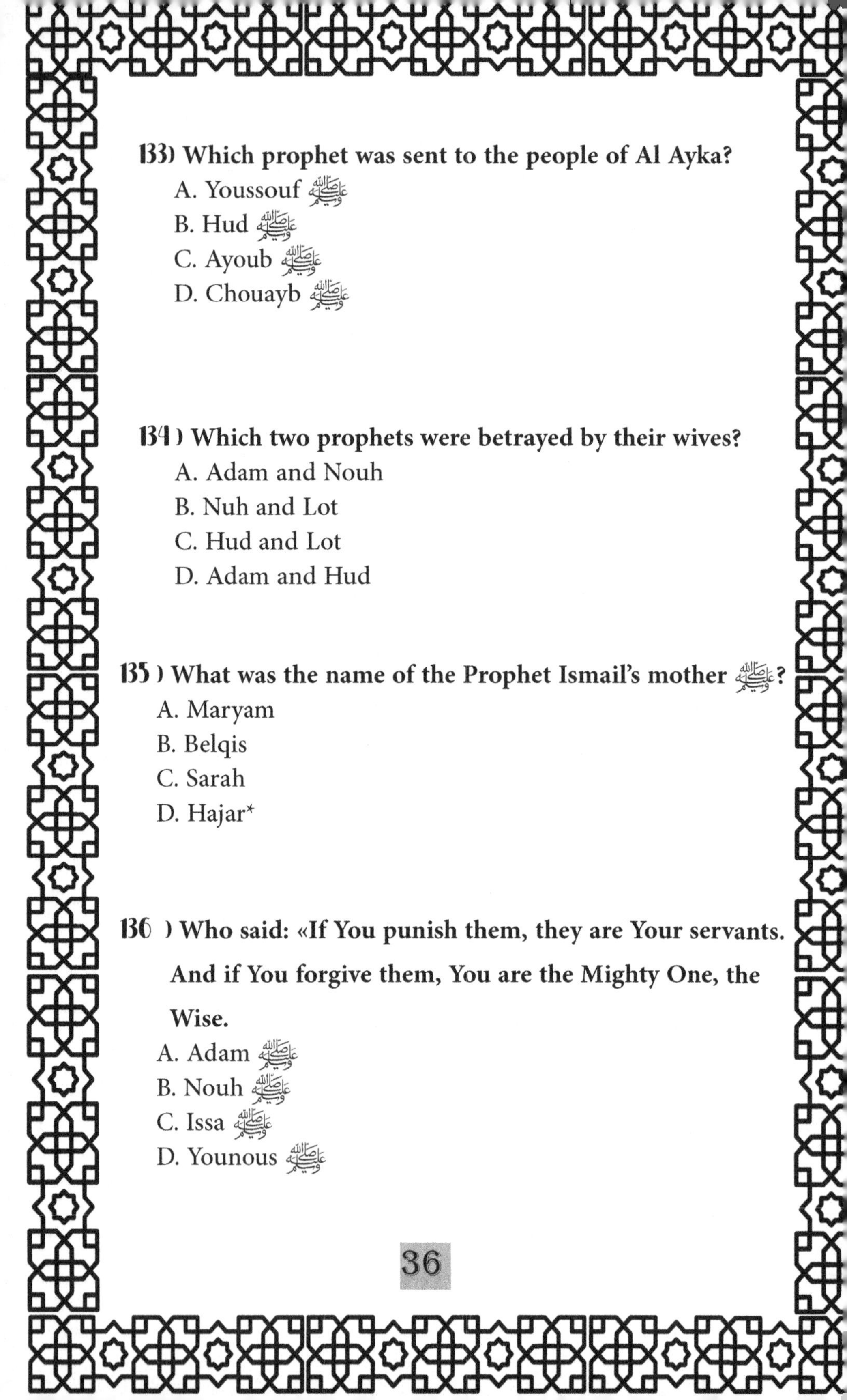

133) Which prophet was sent to the people of Al Ayka?

A. Youssouf ﷺ
B. Hud ﷺ
C. Ayoub ﷺ
D. Chouayb ﷺ

134) Which two prophets were betrayed by their wives?

A. Adam and Nouh
B. Nuh and Lot
C. Hud and Lot
D. Adam and Hud

135) What was the name of the Prophet Ismail's mother ﷺ?

A. Maryam
B. Belqis
C. Sarah
D. Hajar*

136) Who said: «If You punish them, they are Your servants. And if You forgive them, You are the Mighty One, the Wise.

A. Adam ﷺ
B. Nouh ﷺ
C. Issa ﷺ
D. Younous ﷺ

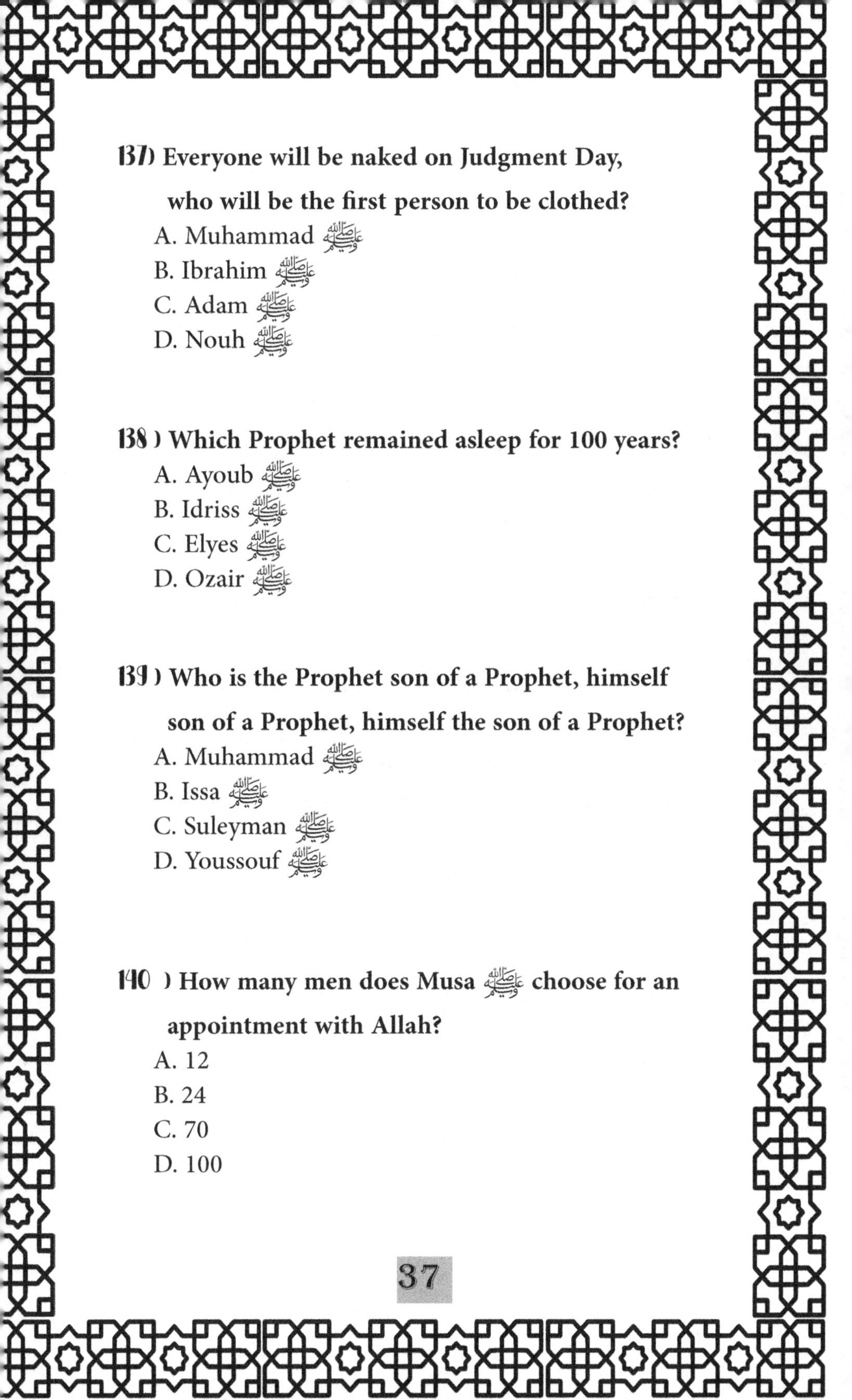

137) Everyone will be naked on Judgment Day, who will be the first person to be clothed?

A. Muhammad صلى الله عليه وسلم
B. Ibrahim صلى الله عليه وسلم
C. Adam صلى الله عليه وسلم
D. Nouh صلى الله عليه وسلم

138) Which Prophet remained asleep for 100 years?

A. Ayoub صلى الله عليه وسلم
B. Idriss صلى الله عليه وسلم
C. Elyes صلى الله عليه وسلم
D. Ozair صلى الله عليه وسلم

139) Who is the Prophet son of a Prophet, himself son of a Prophet, himself the son of a Prophet?

A. Muhammad صلى الله عليه وسلم
B. Issa صلى الله عليه وسلم
C. Suleyman صلى الله عليه وسلم
D. Youssouf صلى الله عليه وسلم

140) How many men does Musa صلى الله عليه وسلم choose for an appointment with Allah?

A. 12
B. 24
C. 70
D. 100

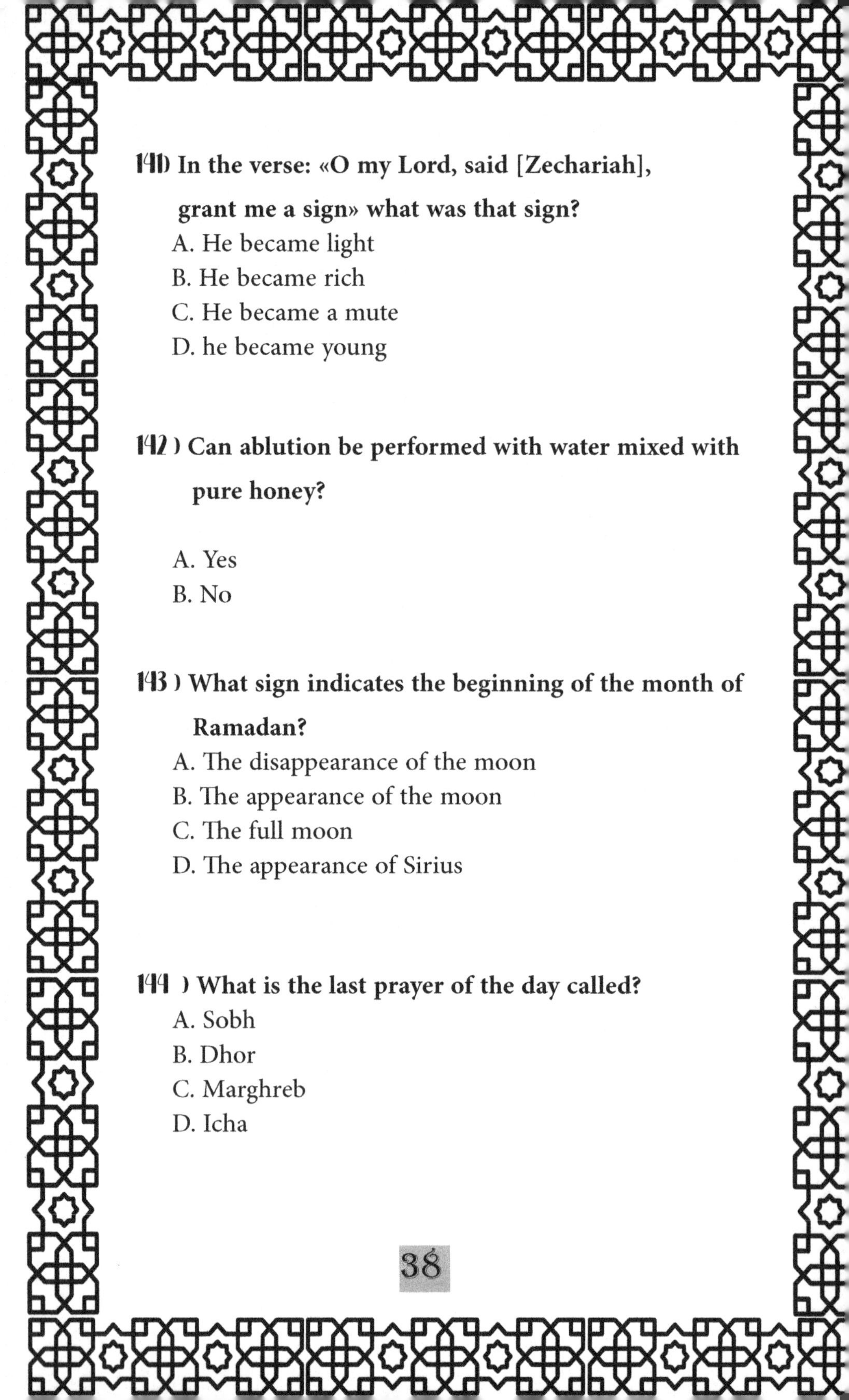

141) In the verse: «O my Lord, said [Zechariah], grant me a sign» what was that sign?

A. He became light
B. He became rich
C. He became a mute
D. he became young

142) Can ablution be performed with water mixed with pure honey?

A. Yes
B. No

143) What sign indicates the beginning of the month of Ramadan?

A. The disappearance of the moon
B. The appearance of the moon
C. The full moon
D. The appearance of Sirius

144) What is the last prayer of the day called?

A. Sobh
B. Dhor
C. Marghreb
D. Icha

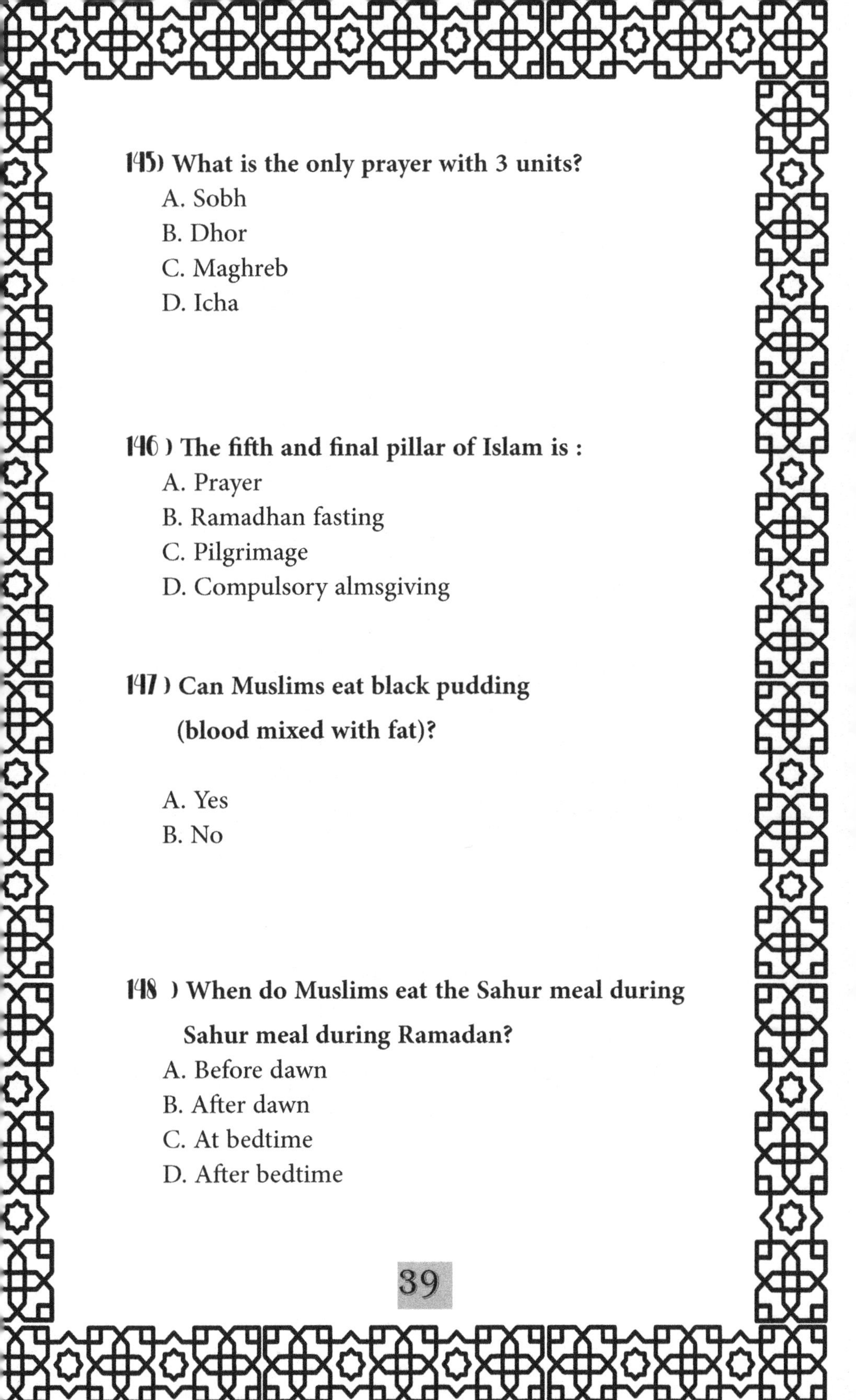

145) What is the only prayer with 3 units?

A. Sobh
B. Dhor
C. Maghreb
D. Icha

146) The fifth and final pillar of Islam is :

A. Prayer
B. Ramadhan fasting
C. Pilgrimage
D. Compulsory almsgiving

147) Can Muslims eat black pudding (blood mixed with fat)?

A. Yes
B. No

148) When do Muslims eat the Sahur meal during Sahur meal during Ramadan?

A. Before dawn
B. After dawn
C. At bedtime
D. After bedtime

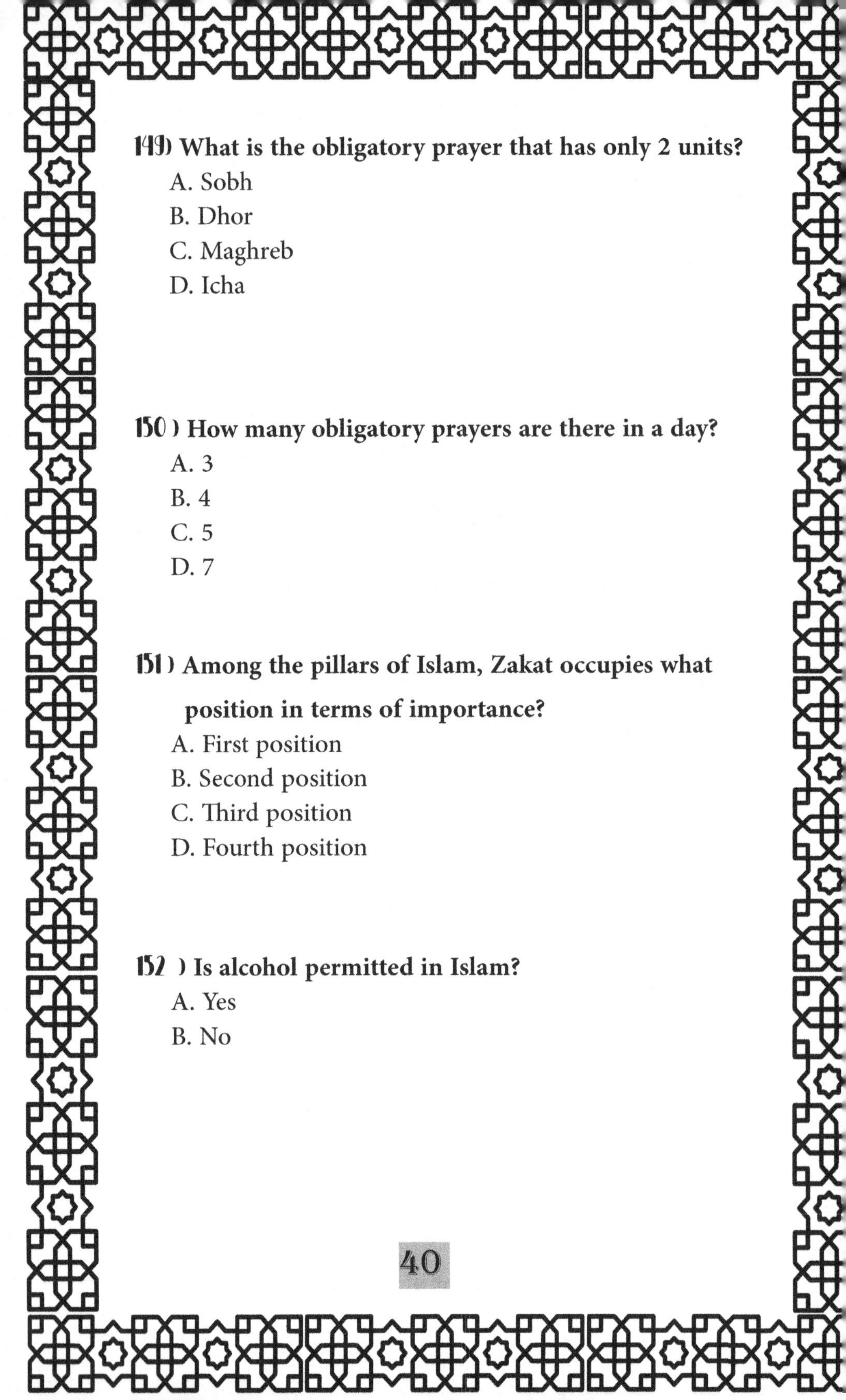

149) What is the obligatory prayer that has only 2 units?

A. Sobh
B. Dhor
C. Maghreb
D. Icha

150) How many obligatory prayers are there in a day?

A. 3
B. 4
C. 5
D. 7

151) Among the pillars of Islam, Zakat occupies what position in terms of importance?

A. First position
B. Second position
C. Third position
D. Fourth position

152) Is alcohol permitted in Islam?

A. Yes
B. No

153) What colour is the pilgrims' clothing during the Hajj?

A. Black
B. White
C. Blue
D. None in particular

154) Fish and all seafood products are forbidden in Islam

A. Yes
B. No

155) When do I get to eat and drink during Ramadan?

A. Dawn
B. The dawn
C. Sunset
D. At night

156) The Ihram, the male pilgrimage garment is composed of how many parts?

A. 1
B. 2
C. 3
D. 4

157) How many categories of people are entitled to receive to receive Zakat?

A. 2
B. 5
C. 8
D. Not defined

158) How long should the surplus of our property be kept of our property to be eligible for zakat?

A. 1 month
B. 6 months
C. 1 year
D. 2 years

159) How many times must the pilgrim make the journey between the two mounts Saffa and Marwah?

A. 0
B. 1
C. 5
D. 7

160) The patient is obliged to fast during the month of of Ramadan?

A. True
B. False

161) What colour is the women's clothing during Hajj?

A. Black
B. White
C. Blue
D. None in particular

162) The levy rate for Zakat Al Mal is :

A. 1%
B. 2%
C. 2.5%
D. 5%

163) In what year of the Hegira did the fasting of the month of Ramadan became obligatory?

A. The 1st year
B. The 2nd year
C. The 3rd year
D. The 4th year

164) «When you read the Quran, start by invoking God's protection against the stoned demon».

A. A hadith
B. A verse
C. A piece of wisdom
D. A poem

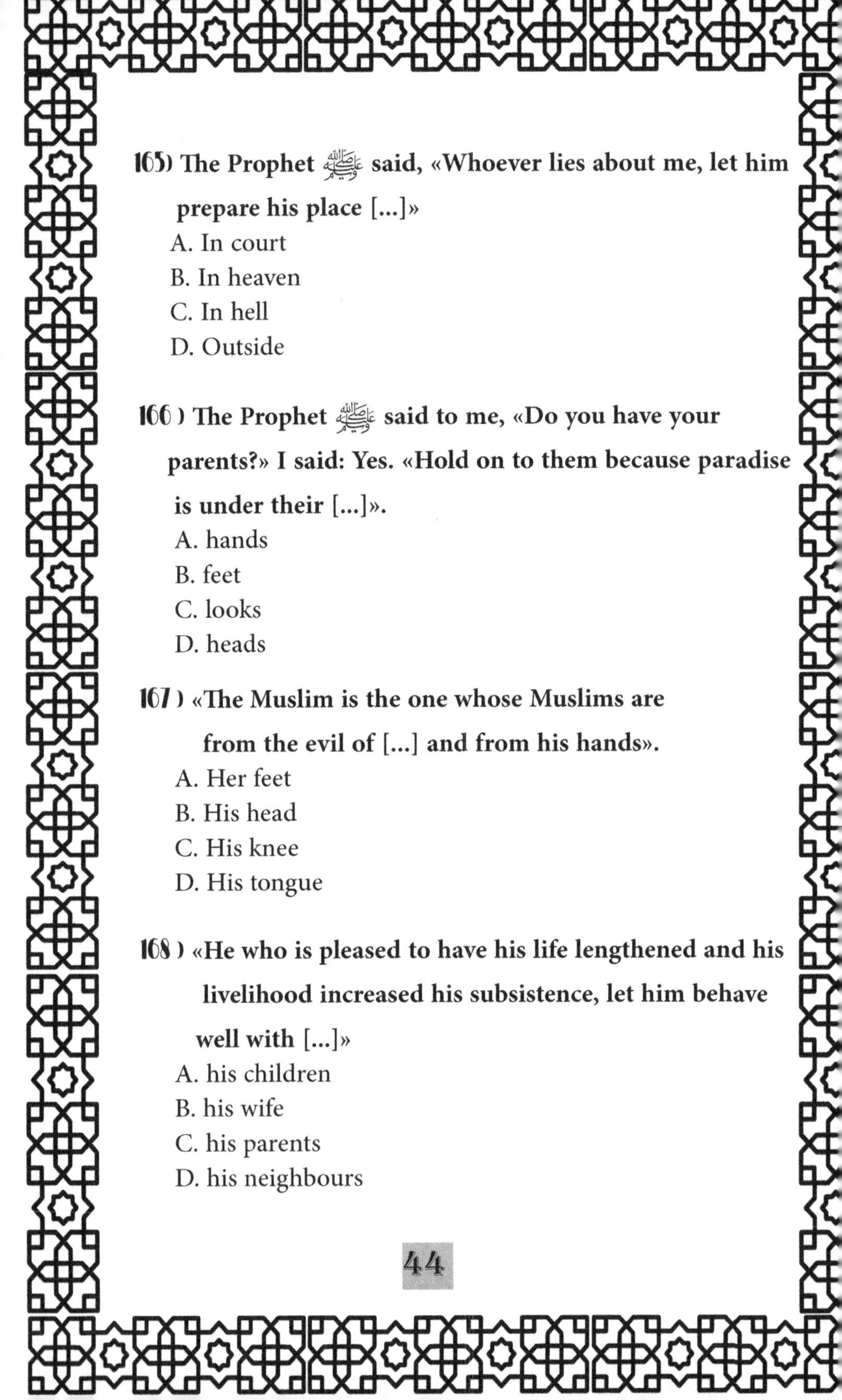

165) The Prophet ﷺ said, «Whoever lies about me, let him prepare his place [...]»

A. In court
B. In heaven
C. In hell
D. Outside

166) The Prophet ﷺ said to me, «Do you have your parents?» I said: Yes. «Hold on to them because paradise is under their [...]».

A. hands
B. feet
C. looks
D. heads

167) «The Muslim is the one whose Muslims are from the evil of [...] and from his hands».

A. Her feet
B. His head
C. His knee
D. His tongue

168) «He who is pleased to have his life lengthened and his livelihood increased his subsistence, let him behave well with [...]»

A. his children
B. his wife
C. his parents
D. his neighbours

169) **Hafsa is the daughter of ?**

A. Abou Bakr
B. Omar
C. Ali
D. Hamza

170) **Who was Hamza the Lion of Allah to the Prophet ﷺ ?**

A. His brother
B. His cousin
C. His nephew
D. His uncle

171) **Who was the cousin of the Prophet ﷺ?**

A. Abdallah Ibn Omar
B. Abdallah Ibn Mas'oud
C. Abdallah Ibn Ommi Maktum
D. Abdallah Ibn Abbas

172) **Who was the fourth rightly guided Caliph of Islam?**

A. Abou Bakr
B. Omar
C. Othman
D. Ali

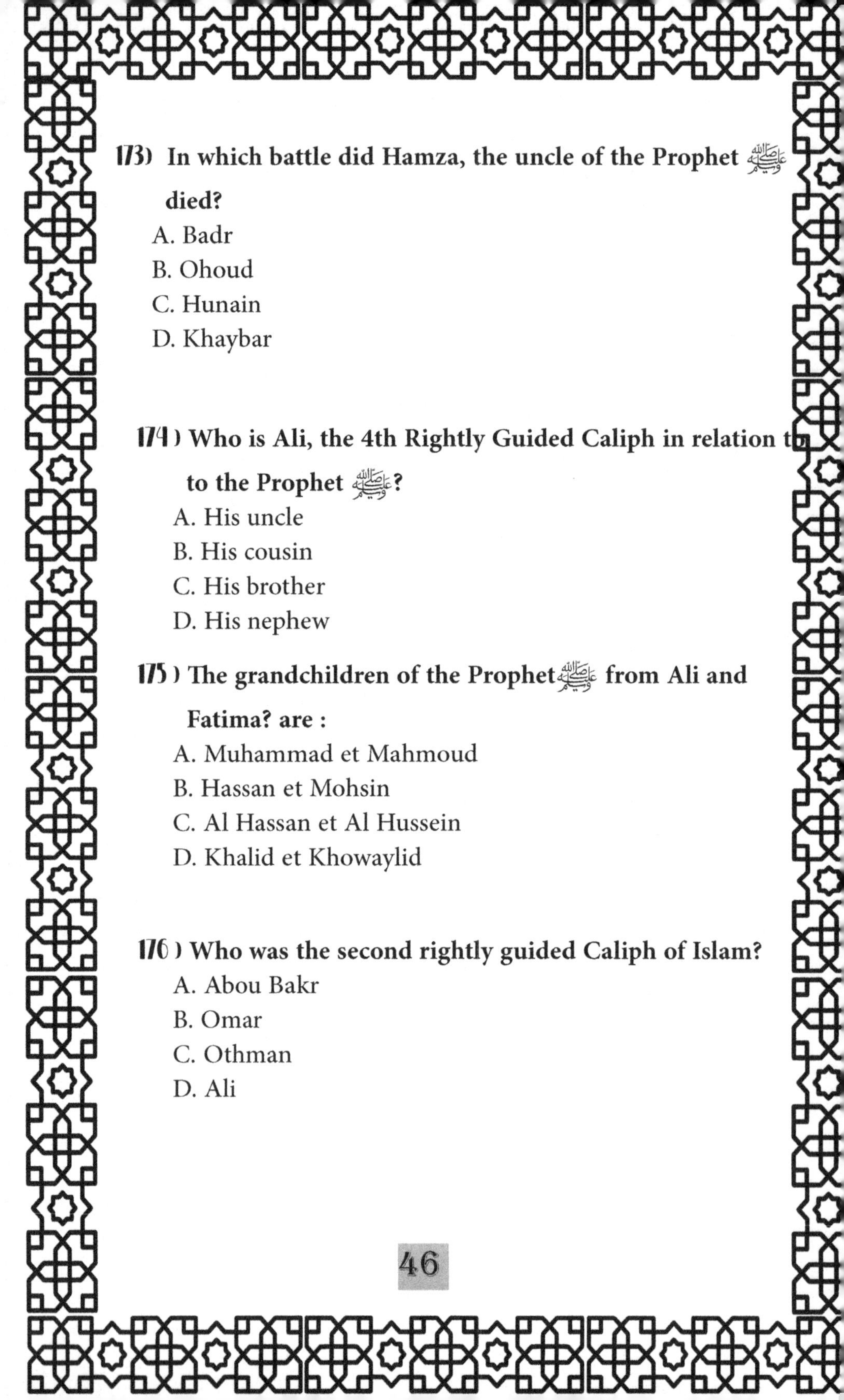

173) In which battle did Hamza, the uncle of the Prophet ﷺ died?

A. Badr
B. Ohoud
C. Hunain
D. Khaybar

174) Who is Ali, the 4th Rightly Guided Caliph in relation to to the Prophet ﷺ?

A. His uncle
B. His cousin
C. His brother
D. His nephew

175) The grandchildren of the Prophet ﷺ from Ali and Fatima? are :

A. Muhammad et Mahmoud
B. Hassan et Mohsin
C. Al Hassan et Al Hussein
D. Khalid et Khowaylid

176) Who was the second rightly guided Caliph of Islam?

A. Abou Bakr
B. Omar
C. Othman
D. Ali

177) Who is not one of the 10 promised to Paradise ?

A. Talha
B. Zubeyr
C. Abou Obayda
D. Abou siffeddine

178) The order of the Rightly Guided Caliphs is Abu Bakr, Umar, Ali and Uthman?

A. True
B. False

179) What is the most practiced religion in the world?

A. Islam
B. Christianity
C. Hinduism
D. Atheism

180) Why did Iblis the cursed refuse to bow down to bow down to Adam ﷺ?

A. Out of jealousy
B. Out of envy
C. Out of pride
D. Out of malice

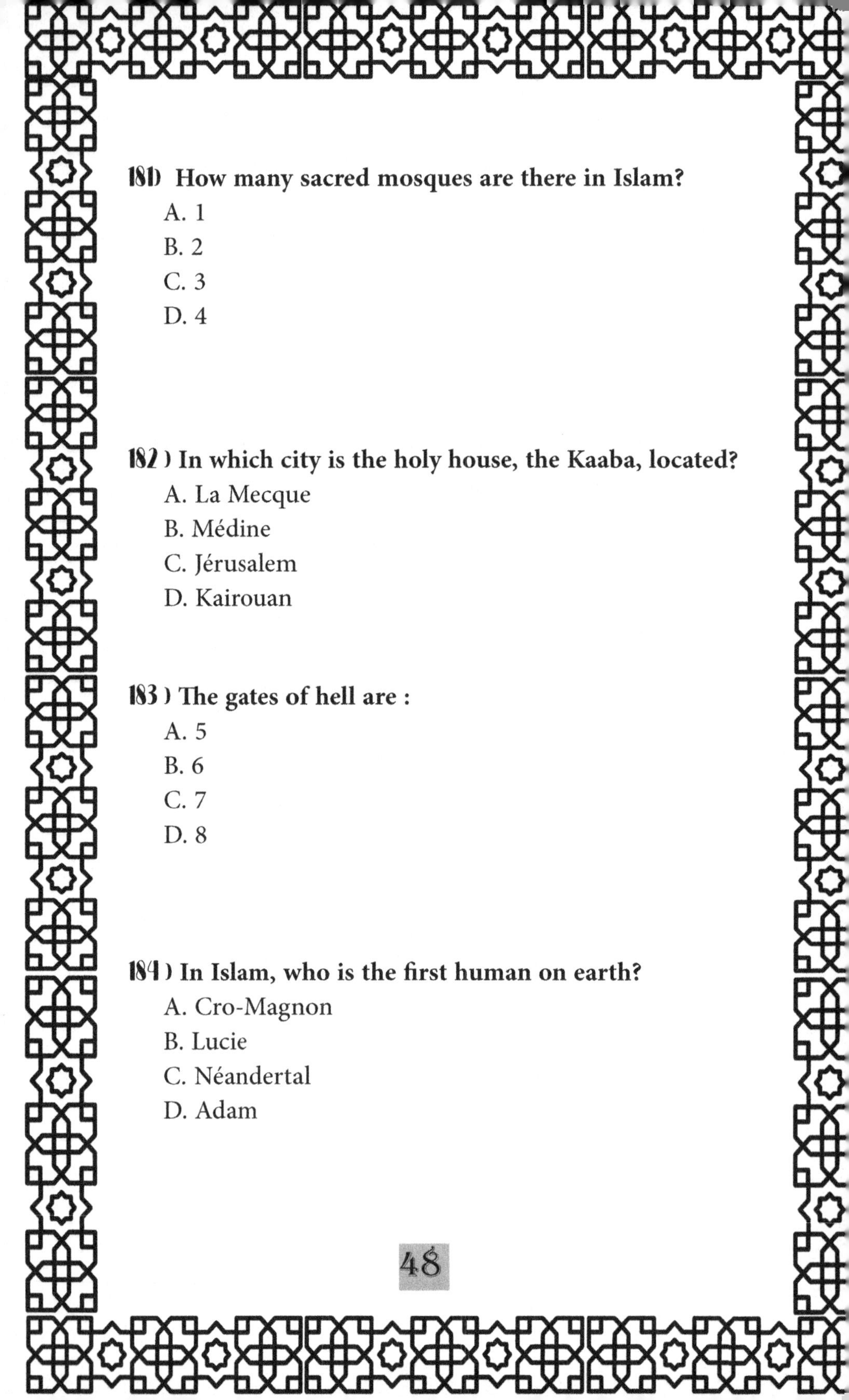

181) How many sacred mosques are there in Islam?

A. 1
B. 2
C. 3
D. 4

182) In which city is the holy house, the Kaaba, located?

A. La Mecque
B. Médine
C. Jérusalem
D. Kairouan

183) The gates of hell are :

A. 5
B. 6
C. 7
D. 8

184) In Islam, who is the first human on earth?

A. Cro-Magnon
B. Lucie
C. Néandertal
D. Adam

185) What is Kiswa?

A. A camel

B. The covering of the Kaaba

C. A garment

D. A prayer

186) In which holy month of the Islamic calendar should the Hajj must be performed?

A. Dhul Q'ida

B. Dhul Hijja

C. Muharram

D. Rajab

187) What does «Salam» mean?

A. Hello

B. Peace

C. Drink

D. Goodbye

188) What is the absolute enemy of humans on Earth?

A. The lion

B. The shark

C. Pollution

D. The Devil

189) Why did one of Adam's two sons kill his brother?

A. Out of jealousy
B. Out of pride
C. Out of love
D. Out of anger

190) A Muslim surgeon who invented more than 200 surgical instruments?

A. Al kindi
B. Avicenne
C. Al Zahrawi
D. Al Bouti

191) The gates of Paradise are :

A. 7
B. 8
C. 10
D. 6

192) What do the fruits of the tree of hell look like «Zaqqum»?

A. Has apples
B. A devil's head
C. A thorns
D. Has dates

193) What is tafsir?

A. A book of Hadith

B. A book of law

C. Ancient tales

D. The explanation of the Qur'an

194) According to Bukhari and Moslim, how many different names does Allah have?

A. 1

B. 33

C. 99

D. 135

195) What is Zabour?

A. A tree of heaven

B. A tree from hell

C. A revealed book

D. An angel

196) How many holy books are there?

A. 1

B. 3

C. 4

D. 5

197) What is the last step before the final entry to Heaven or Hell?

A. The judgment
B. The Hawd Basin
C. The Sirat Bridge
D. The scales

198) What is the name of the garment worn by the faithful during the Hajj?

A. Qamis
B. Ihram
C. Kittan
D. Hijjah

199) Which people succeeded the people of Nuh ﷺ?

A. ‘Ad
B. Thamud
C. Maydan
D. Tubba

200) There are three things that follow the dead, two return and only one remains, what is the thing that remains with him?

A. His property
B. His family
C. His actions
D. His word

201) How many verses does the Quran contain?

A. 6235
B. 6237
C. 6236
D. 6000

202) Who were the first converts to Islam?

A. Khadija, Ali, Abu Bakr, Zeid
B. Khadija, the companions, Abu Bakr
C. The companions
D. Ali

203) How many days are recommended for fasting per week and what are they?

A. 4: Monday, Wednesday, Friday and Sunday
B. 3: Tuesday, Thursday and Saturday
C. 2: Monday and Thursday
D. 1: Friday

204) Who are the 2 most famous Hadith reporters in in Islam?

A. Muslim and At-Tirmidhi
B. Al-Bukhari and Al-Bayhaqi
C. Al-Bukhari and Muslim
D. Al-Bayhaqi and At-Tirmidhi

205) What should Muslims do during the month of of Ramadan?

A. Fasting from dawn to sunset
B. Reading the Qur'an
C. Giving to the poor
D. All of the above

206) Which country has the largest number of number of Muslims?

A. Iran
B. Indonesia
C. Turkey
D. Iraq

207) Muslims represent what proportion of the world population?

A. 5 %
B. 23 %
C. 33 %
D. 48 %

208) Which of these Muslim-majority countries is not part of the 'Arab world'?

A. Iran
B. Yemen
C. Tunisia
D. Algeria

209) Who is the first Messenger sent by God Almighty to mankind?

A. Mousa ﷺ
B. Nooh ﷺ
C. Idris ﷺ
D. Adam ﷺ

210) What is the prayer in which there is no bowing or prostration?

A. Prayers for rain
B. The Aid prayer
C. Funeral prayer
D. Prayer of Fear

211) Is Allah ﷻ alive? or a condition for his existence?

A. Allah is Alive and does not need food and water
B. Allah is alive and does not depend on anything
C. Allah is Alive and depends on the worship of creatures
D. It is not known whether Allah is Alive

212) Is Allah ﷻ subject to drowsiness or sleep?

A. To drowsiness yes, but not to sleep
B. To sleep yes , but not to drowsiness
C. Allah does not sleep and does not doze
D. Yes to drowsiness and sleep

213) After the death of the Prophet , what to say if a a person presents himself, pretending to be a prophet, working miracles?

A. If he walks on the sea, then he is a prophet
B. If he raises the dead, then he is a prophet
C. There can be no prophet after Muhammad (ﷺ)
D. Nothing is impossible!

214) The Quran was revealed during ?

A. 10 years
B. 13 years
C. 23 years
D. 27 years

215) What is the first word in the book of the Quran?

A. Bismillah
B. El Hamdoulilah
C. Iqra
D. Alif Lam Mim

216) Can the human imagination represent Allah?

A. Humans no, but Djinns yes
B. Humans no, but Angels yes
C. No imagination can represent Him
D. Of course

217) The greatest Sura of the Quran

A. The cow Al Baqarah
B. The family of Imrane
C. Surah Ibrahim
D. Surah the Cave

218) The Sura that does not contain the letter Mim

A. The dawn - Al Falaq
B. The People - Al Nass
C. Sincerity - Al Ikhlass
D. Abundance -Al Kawthar

219) The summer journey of the Qoraich was to the Cham and the winter journey was to ?

A. Abyssinia
B. Oman
C. Bahrain
D. Yemen

220) Where do the Hawamim suras begin?

A. Alif Lam Mim
B. Alim Lam Mim Ra
C. Ha Mim
D. Ta Sin

221) What is the characteristic of a religion monotheistic ?

A. There is only one Imâm
B. There is only one God
C. There is only one Prophet
D. There are three gods

222) To those who do good is reserved the best (reward) and even more . What does refers to?

A. The Vision of Allah
B. Eternal Life
C. Escape from hell
D. The Houris (women of paradise)

223) What does Îmân mean?

A. Submission to Allah
B. Faith
C. Purity
D. Peace

224) What does «Bismillâhi Ar - Rahmâni Ar - Rahîm»?

A. Allah, Lord of the universe
B. Praise be to Allah, Lord of the universe
C. The Most Gracious, the Most Merciful
D. In the name of Allah, the Most Gracious, the Most Merciful

225) What words should a Muslim say when he is dying (before his death)?

A. Al - Hamdu Lillâh
B. Lâ ilâha illâ - Llah
C. Je vais certainement mourir
D. Astaghfiru - Llâh

226) The beginning of the Muslim calendar is approximately on what date?

A. July 522
B. January 622
C. July 622
D. January 522

227) What is the status of learning science for every Muslim?

A. Easy
B. Optional
C. An obligation
D. Difficult

228) The reward of the woman who performs her prayers, fasts in the month of Ramadan, preserves her chastity her chastity and obeys her husband is that she will enter In what way will she enter Paradise?

A. Through any door she wants
B. By the door of the pious
C. By the door of the Houris
D. Through the door of the Pure

229) **What is the name of the tower at the top of the mosque from which the muezzin makes the Adhân (announcement the entrance of the prayer time)?**

A. A minaret
B. A minbar
C. A roof
D. None of the above

230) **What are these two benefits that many people do not people don't fully appreciate?**

A. Health and leisure time
B. Health and money
C. Food and youth
D. Health

231) **The Prophet (ﷺ) cited which act as completing half of the religion?**

A. Almsgiving
B. Good behaviour
C. Recitation of Surah al - Ikhlâs
D. Marriage

232) **Who committed the first murder of all mankind?**

A. One of the sons of Nuh (Noah)
B. A fast of the people of Lût (Lot)
C. As-Samirî
D. One of the sons of Âdam

233) **From what material are angels created?**

A. Fire
B. Light
C. Clay
D. Crystal

234) **From what matter are the Djinns created?**

A. Clay
B. Light
C. Mixture of clay and light
D. Fire

235) **What should be the priority in the choice of of a wife?**

A. Her beauty
B. Religion
C. Wealth
D. His diploma

236) **What do we call the Muslims of Mecca who were welcomed by the Muslims of Medina?**

A. The Muhajirûn
B. The Ansâr
C. The Musâfirûn
D. The Mujâhid

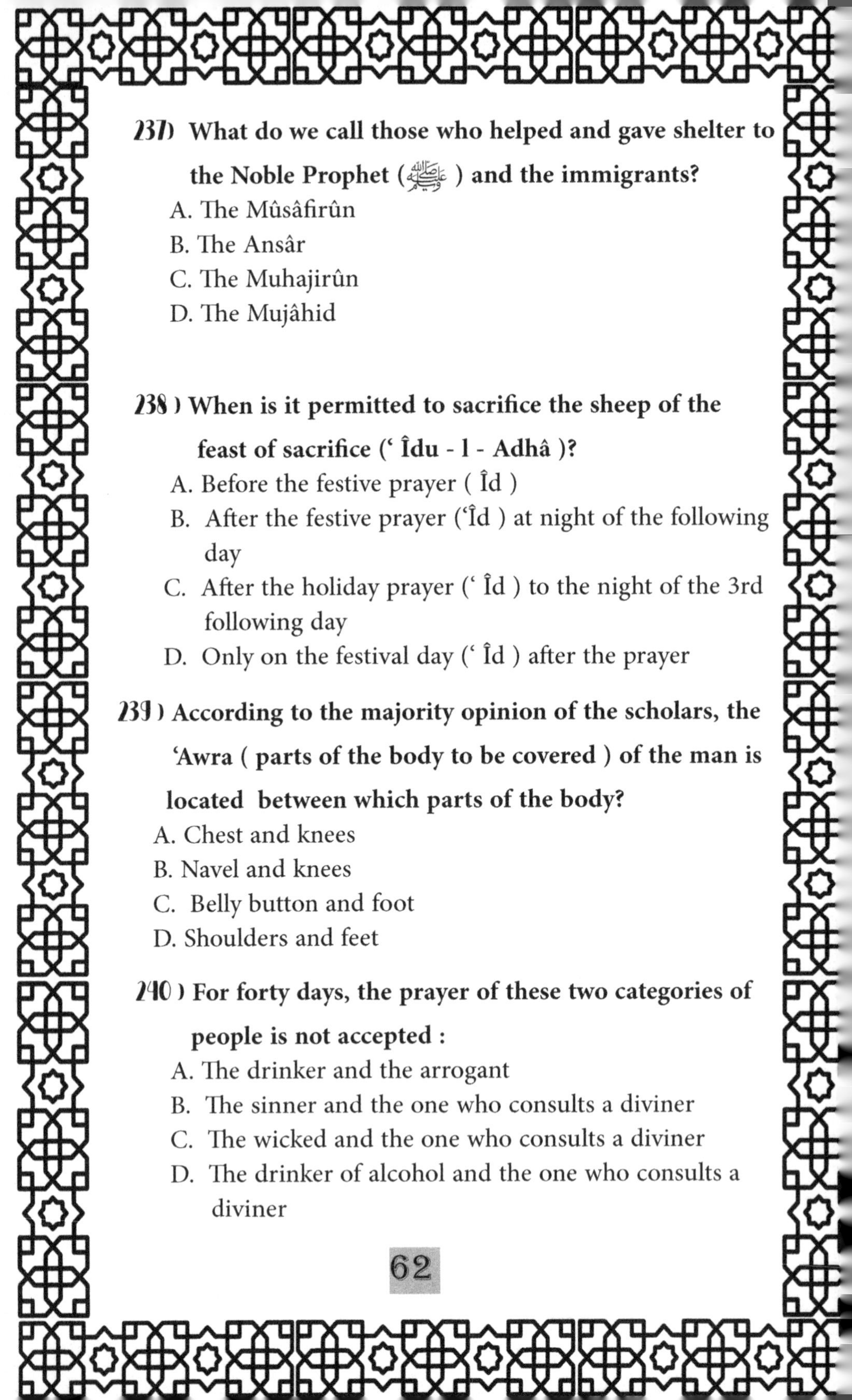

237) What do we call those who helped and gave shelter to the Noble Prophet (ﷺ) and the immigrants?

A. The Mûsâfirûn

B. The Ansâr

C. The Muhajirûn

D. The Mujâhid

238) When is it permitted to sacrifice the sheep of the feast of sacrifice (' Îdu - l - Adhâ)?

A. Before the festive prayer (Îd)

B. After the festive prayer ('Îd) at night of the following day

C. After the holiday prayer (' Îd) to the night of the 3rd following day

D. Only on the festival day (' Îd) after the prayer

239) According to the majority opinion of the scholars, the 'Awra (parts of the body to be covered) of the man is located between which parts of the body?

A. Chest and knees

B. Navel and knees

C. Belly button and foot

D. Shoulders and feet

240) For forty days, the prayer of these two categories of people is not accepted :

A. The drinker and the arrogant

B. The sinner and the one who consults a diviner

C. The wicked and the one who consults a diviner

D. The drinker of alcohol and the one who consults a diviner

241) What does Sunna mean?

A. The words and deeds of the Companions
B. All the rules from the Qur'an
C. The sayings and deeds and approvals of the Prophet (ﷺ)
D. All these propositions

242) What are the places most loved and most hated by Allah ﷻ?

A. Loved: village, hated: markets
B. Loved: cities, hated: markets
C. Loved: mosques, hated: toilets
D. Loved: mosques , hated: markets

243) What does the term Bid'a mean?

A. New technologies
B. Opinion on religion
C. Innovation in everything
D. Innovation in religion

244) How many wings does the angel Jibril have?

A. 4
B. 100
C. 200
D. 600

245) He to whom Allah ﷻ wishes good, he ... ?

A. Grants him wealth

B. Instructs him in religion

C. Grant him poverty

D. Makes him intelligent

246) The legal clothing of the Muslim woman must hide her whole body except ?

A. The head

B. Face and hands

C. Feet and head

D. Knee to foot

247) What are the two most beloved names of Allah?

A. ' Abdallah and ' Abd Ar - Rahmân

B. Muhammad and ' Abd Ar - Rahmân

C. Muhammad and ' Abdallah

D. Ibrâhîm and ' Abd Ar - Rahmân

248) Approximately how many days are there in a in a year of the Muslim calendar (lunar calendar)?

A. 350

B. 354

C. 365

D. 366

249) Good deeds can be multiplied

up to ... ?

A. 70 times

B. 250 times

C. 500 times

D. 700 times

250) What do we call the period before Islam?

A. Al - Inhilâl

B. At - Tafasukh

C. Al - Jâhiliyya

D. Al - Wathaniyya

251) Who was the leader of the hypocrites of Medina?

A. Khalid b . al - Walîd

B. Abû Jahl

C. Abû Sufyân b . Harb

D. ‘Abdullah b . Ubayy

252) What are the 4 holy months in Islam?

A. Dhû - l - Qi'da , Dhû - l - Hijja , Muharram et Chawwâl

B. Dhû - l - Qi'da , Dhû - l - Hijja , Muharram et Ramadân

C. Dhû - l - Qi'da , Dhû - l - Hijja ,Ramadân , Rajab

D. Dhû - l - Qi'da , Dhû - l - Hijja , Muharram et Rajab

253) How many days are there in a month of the Muslim calendar (Hegira)?

A. 29 or 30
B. 29
C. 28 or 29
D. 30 or 31

254) What are the names of the four Sunni schools?

A. Hanafite , Mâlikite , Châfi'îte , Médinite
B. Hanafite , Mâlikite , Mecquite , Chrite
C. Hanafite , Mâlikite , Chrite Châfi'îte
D. Hanafite , Mâlikite , Châfi'îte , Hanbalite

255) What is the name of the angel in charge of rain and vegetation?

A. Mikâl (Mikail)
B. Isrâfîl
C. Ridwân
D. Jibril (Gabriel)

Responses

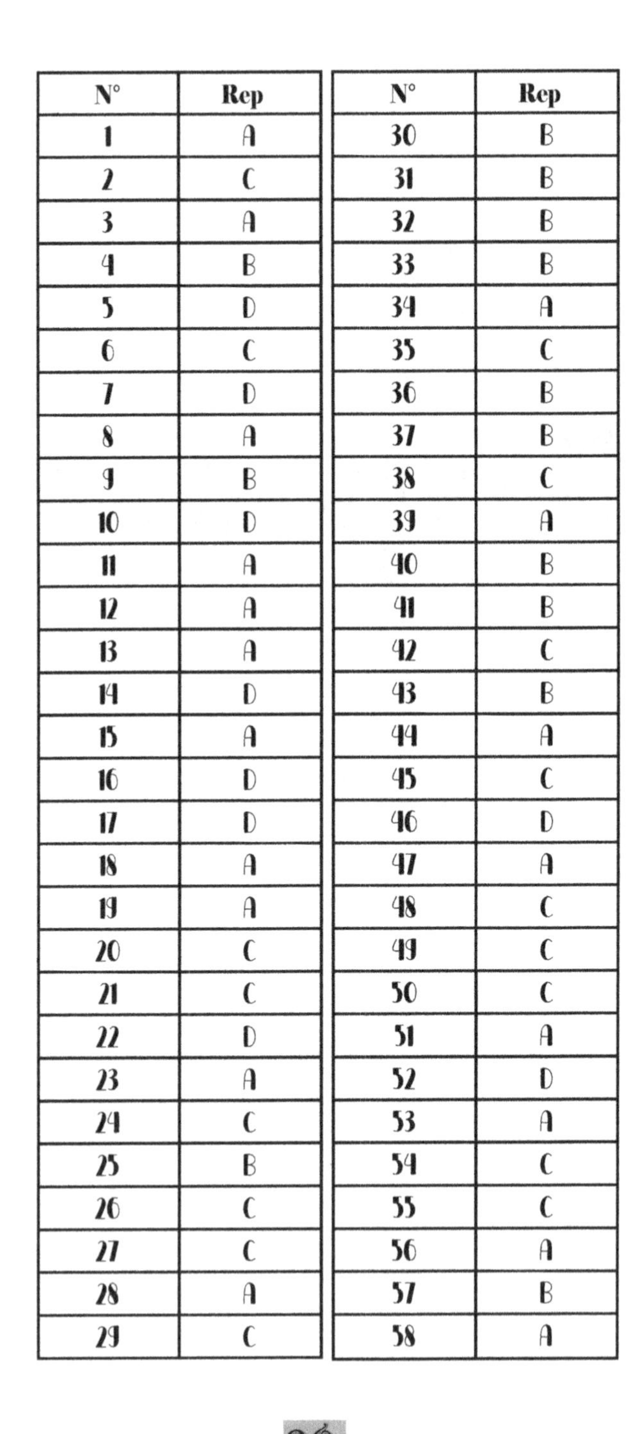

N°	Rep	N°	Rep
1	A	30	B
2	C	31	B
3	A	32	B
4	B	33	B
5	D	34	A
6	C	35	C
7	D	36	B
8	A	37	B
9	B	38	C
10	D	39	A
11	A	40	B
12	A	41	B
13	A	42	C
14	D	43	B
15	A	44	A
16	D	45	C
17	D	46	D
18	A	47	A
19	A	48	C
20	C	49	C
21	C	50	C
22	D	51	A
23	A	52	D
24	C	53	A
25	B	54	C
26	C	55	C
27	C	56	A
28	A	57	B
29	C	58	A

N°	Rep	N°	Rep
59	B	88	C
60	C	89	B
61	D	90	D
62	C	91	A
63	A	92	C
64	A	93	D
65	D	94	B
66	C	95	A
67	D	96	B
68	C	97	B
69	B	98	A
70	A	99	B
71	C	100	A
72	A	101	B
73	A	102	B
74	A	103	C
75	A	104	C
76	C	105	C
77	A	106	C
78	D	107	A
79	A	108	D
80	C	109	C
81	A	110	B
82	B	111	B
83	C	112	A
84	A	113	C
85	B	114	A
86	D	115	B
87	B	116	C

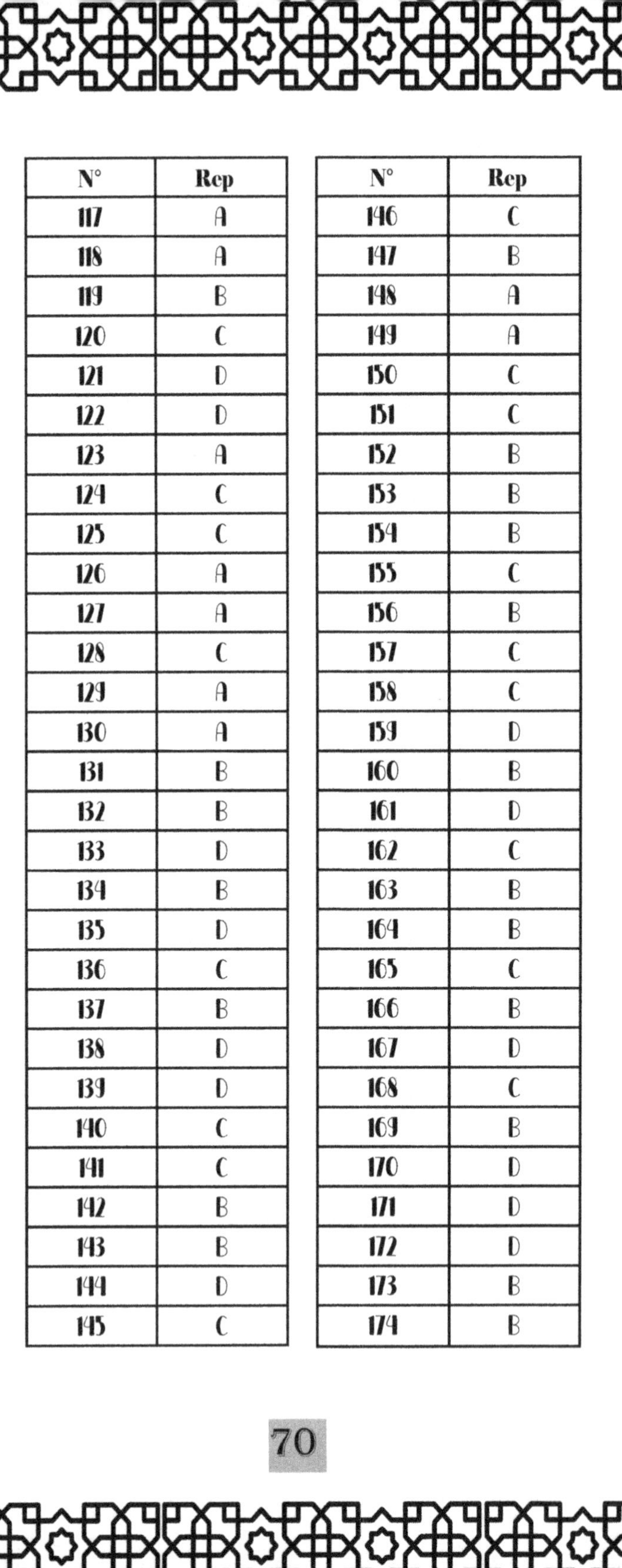

N°	Rep
117	A
118	A
119	B
120	C
121	D
122	D
123	A
124	C
125	C
126	A
127	A
128	C
129	A
130	A
131	B
132	B
133	D
134	B
135	D
136	C
137	B
138	D
139	D
140	C
141	C
142	B
143	B
144	D
145	C

N°	Rep
146	C
147	B
148	A
149	A
150	C
151	C
152	B
153	B
154	B
155	C
156	B
157	C
158	C
159	D
160	B
161	D
162	C
163	B
164	B
165	C
166	B
167	D
168	C
169	B
170	D
171	D
172	D
173	B
174	B

N°	Rep
175	C
176	B
177	D
178	B
179	A
180	C
181	C
182	A
183	C
184	D
185	B
186	B
187	B
188	D
189	A
190	C
191	B
192	B
193	D
194	C
195	C
196	D
197	C
198	B
199	A
200	C
201	C
202	A
203	C

N°	Rep
204	C
205	D
206	B
207	B
208	A
209	B
210	C
211	B
212	C
213	C
214	C
215	A
216	C
217	A
218	D
219	D
220	C
221	B
222	A
223	B
224	D
225	B
226	C
227	C
228	A
229	A
230	A
231	D
232	D

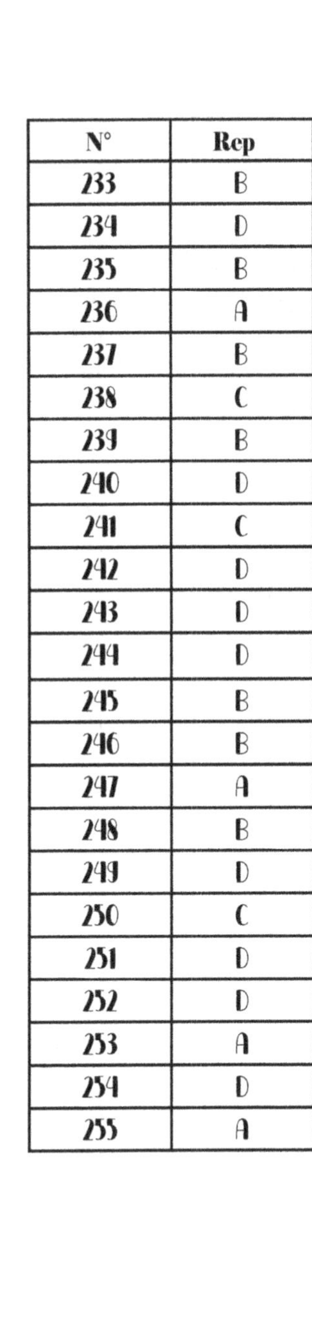

N°	Rep
233	B
234	D
235	B
236	A
237	B
238	C
239	B
240	D
241	C
242	D
243	D
244	D
245	B
246	B
247	A
248	B
249	D
250	C
251	D
252	D
253	A
254	D
255	A

Notes :

Made in United States
Orlando, FL
07 May 2023